Caesar Productions Presents…

Lyrical Thoughts

&

Stories

Volume 1

Caesar Productions Presents… Lyrical Thoughts

&

Stories

"From an artist perspective, when you painting a picture, you have to use the colors. If you want it to feel the way things feel in the environment, you have to use the slang, the terminology that applies" – 50 Cent

This is my introduction to Lyrical Thoughts & Stories. It's a collection of stories that are written in rhyme form. I used to write rhymes when I was a teenager, that passion that I had for Hip Hop never died. As time went on, I stopped writing rhymes and decided to start a family in 1996. This was the first time that I had stopped writing since I was 13. I wrote Teenage Love in 1997, and it was a true story of some friends I had back in New York. That was my first "Lyrical Story". It was a great story, but I thought it was a onetime thing. Then one night in 2002 when I was working the night shift at the Post Office, I just had gotten overcome with a rush of lyrics that I just had to write down. It was coming so fast that I grabbed the nearest pen and paper and started jotting it down before I forgot it.

That night I wrote "I Can't Remember To Forget You", one of my favorite stories. From there I went on a writing spree, writing full stories every night it seemed. But every story was in the form of a rap, but just longer. The words and slang that I use in most of my stories are the same words that are prevalent in Hip Hop. Even though the language might seem improper, it just to emphasize the situations. The words might seem harsh at times, but it's real.

Dedication

I want to dedicate this book to three people that have greatly influenced my life. My wife, Jessica for always holding me down and giving me that extra push when I needed it. For always having my back and helping me see the bigger picture when my frustration gets the best of me. I love you, always. To my Mother Darlia "Dee" McFall, who was always that supporting system for her four children, no matter what we wanted to do, she was there pushing us along with constructive criticism and humor. I miss you every day. This book wouldn't even be a possibility if it weren't for my late Grand-Father William "Lucky" McFall. His lyrical skill to just come up with rhymes off of the top of his head was just immaculate. His lyricism has filtered down to his children and grandchildren, who uses that skill for various things. The ultimate family man and consummate showman, if I end up being just half of the man you were, I'd be blessed. I love and miss you too.

This book is for you.

Voice Mail

Well, today's the day that I've been dreading all summer,

I have to front like its cool, but everyone knows that I want her,

Not to go, but you know, it's for the best, they suggest,

I roll with the punches but it's gonna be putting my relationship to the test,

Ok, whatever, is my daily response to those pessimists,

Like the love my girl and I have won't be able to make it through this,

I jump in my car and head toward the airport, speeding,

Knowing every bit of any extra time with her is what I'm needing,

Thinking about the past and how her friends said it wouldn't last,

And how I knew from the start that I'd end up loving you fast,

40 miles later I'm getting frisked by an overzealous wand guy,

I'm taking off all kinds of stuff but dude won't even let me by,

Finally I'm loose, running to the United Airlines terminal,

Flight 175 from Boston to Los Angeles? Yup that's where I go,

I see a silhouette of a young woman with long curly hair,

Beautiful legs and out of the window she continues to stare,

Oblivious to her surroundings, it seems she has a lot on her mind,

Her body language is sending signals that she's not doing fine,

I stop running, and sneak up behind her and wrap my arms around her waist,

Walk her closer to the window so that we can see the reflections of each other's face,

As I kiss the back of her neck I catch the familiar scent of her hair,

It's intoxicating, and has me wishing to be anywhere else but here,

I slowly whisper in her ear "I want to thank you for the last two years,"

"More up's than downs, more smiles & laughs than tears,"

"More days together than nights apart,"

"Knowing that I found someone special equals less aches in my heart,"

"Not knowing how I going manage if you step on that plane,"

"Even though it's for the best, this has to be the sweetest pain,"

"If you love something let it go, if it returns, it's meant to be,"

"That's what they say, we'll see, I already found the one that's meant for me,"

The bright sun outside made her tears reflect off the glass ever so clearly,

That I increase the pressure around her waist, I wish I could keep her near me,

She turns around and buries her head deep inside my chest,

Silent tears roll down her face onto her chin, and then fall into the crease of her breast,

Steadily increasing the stress in my heart and the ever growing lump in my throat,

I'm drowning in a sea of heartache trying my best to stay afloat,

I asked her "Am I selfish for not wanting you to go?"

With the a look that I've grown to love, she glances up and says "No"

But you know what's ironic? This was all my idea,

To put her on the path of her dreams and to jumpstart her career,

By giving her a chance at what she wants, I'm giving up what I need,

The best friend I ever had, my future wife, true indeed,

It seems like all of our plans ended up with us walking up the aisle holding hands,

Swimming in crystal waters, romantic strolls at dusk on warm black sand,

Warm tropic wind, gently blowing and caressing her skin,

So many fruity drinks in coconut shells with umbrellas, don't know where to begin,

But time for reality, as they call for her flight,

Damn what would I give to have just one more night,

We slowly walk towards her luggage as people begin to check in,

My hearts beating faster even though it's what I've been expecting,

We exchange looks of uncertainty as I kiss her on her cheek,

With tears in her eyes, her voice trembles as she tries to speak,

"I want to now thank you for encouraging me to follow my dreams,"

"Even though it means we'll be apart for a while so it seems,"

"You know there's nothing more I want than to just spend time with you,"

"And you also that being a lawyer is something I've always wanted to do,"

"But before I could go off to school, I met you, the love of my life,"

"So baby, take this to heart coming from your future wife,"

"I love you with all that I am, every part of my being,"

"Me without you is a life I'm not tempted on seeing,"

"We proved them all wrong, those who said it wouldn't last for too long,"

"Emblazoned on my heart and soul are the words to our very first song,"

"If This World Were Mine, word for word, line for line,"

"We were destine to be together forever in due time,"

The lady at the desk takes her ticket, scans it and checks her in,

This is the precise moment where my loneliness and borderline depression sets in,

"So this is it," I said as my eyes start tearing up as I fix her coat,

Can barely swallow due to the lump of heartache sitting in my throat,

"Yeah," she said, "I'll call you later as soon as I touch down,"

"Or maybe I'll try to sneak in a call 30,000 feet above ground,"

Then we embrace and kissed and at that very moment, everything was fine,

No more stressing about her leaving, no more sorrow, I was fine,

"Ok baby," I said "I love you and look forward to hearing from you,"

"If I'm not home, call my cell and leave a message, it'll do,"

"I love you so much more than words can ever explain,"

"And by the look of the lady holding you ticket, you might wanna get on the plane,"

That gets a laugh from my baby as it breaks the thickness of a somber mood,

With familiar quick wits she starts cracking jokes about the food,

And giving me crap about my Yankees, and how they're going to choke in the next game,

I tell her that I'll be home watching it, and I'm sure the Red Sox will be doing the same,

She laughs and one last kiss is exchanged between the two of us,

It's like we're putting on a show, but really it's nothing new to us,

She walks down the tunnel and everything seemed to turn into slow motion,

For her every step was a glide, no longer walking, it seemed like she was floating,

She has such a confident strut that it shows with every step,

The cool way she puts her hair over her shoulder would make a model feel inept,

Right before I lose sight of her she gives me a wink and a silent I Love You,

And just like that she was gone, and I couldn't return the same I Love You,

I walk to the nearest window to see if I could see her on the plane,

If I could, I'd get arrested because I'd childishly be screaming her name,

But I can't so there won't be any yelling coming from me,

I'll just see the plane off, head home and wait for her call ever so desperately,

So now I'm walking to the exit of the airport, very slow and broken hearted,

Giving her a chance to follow her dreams is something that I hope I started,

I make my way out the building and start the journey back home,

No luggage, no gifts or girl, I'm headed there alone,

I hop in the car and make my way out of the maze they call a parking lot,

Hit the tail end of rush hour, not caring, eager to start a life alone, I'm not,

Sitting in my car reminiscing about all the things we used to do,

Places we used to go, now I'm thinking how I'm going to make it through,

To some I might seem soft and completely whipped over this girl,

But they don't know love like I know love, and for her I'd give the world,

My cell's showing no signal no service so I can't call any friends,

Soon as I get in some sort of range, I'm gonna try to make amends,

And apologize for my ways and actions on the days prior to this,

Before she even left I was missing my girl's kiss,

I make the exit off the highway to make my way back home,

I might even call in tonight; I just kinda want to be alone,

Not surrounded by co-workers and all the drama and latest gossip,

Half the time it doesn't concern them, so I often ask them "Why trip?"

Anyway, breakfast at Mickey D's is almost over so I get an Egg Mc Muffin and hash browns,

A large orange juice and continue on my way downtown,

My cell phone beeps and it shows that I have mail,

Damn, I shouldn't have gotten the food so late; the hash browns look kinda stale,

I wonder if that could be my girl, and I'd check it as I drive,

But it's hard to do that, hold the juice, drive and still make it home alive,

So I'll wait and ignore it and just check it when I get in,

To hear her soft, pretty and sweet voice is what I'll be expecting,

About a half hour later I'm home and turn on the television,

Turn to MTV and go and get some snacks out of the kitchen,

They're playing Jay-Z's newest video H to the Izzo,

I guess because his album dropped today, after the video they show his promo,

Then it all cut off and the VJ comes in and explains,

That the World Trade Center has just been hit by a plane,

I hurried into the living room to see what was the deal,

They actually show live footage of the flames, and I'm thinking "Is this for real?"

I turn to CNN, NBC, MSNBC,

Trying to find out what the hell is going on in NYC,

Reports at this time are sketchy and I'm franticly switching channels,

But I end up on NBC, just sitting there trying to handle,

That a plane just hit one of the twin towers, man its crazy,

The thickest, blackest smoke just rose so fast it just amazes me,

Like how in the hell could a pilot hit a big building like that,

You often hear about fatigue among pilots but come on, a building like that?

The newscaster said that the plane hit the first tower around 8:45,

And I'm thinking it's safe to say that everyone on that flight had died,

People are going crazy in the streets of New York,

With good reason I'd say, then I'd start having crazy thoughts,

Of the plane that crashed, could that have been my girl's flight,

Nah, she was on a straight trip so I'm guessing she's alright,

More time passes and from the angle of the live camera I can see another plane,

Coming in low and smashes into the second building and coming out a ball of flame,

I yell out "WHAT THE HELL IS GOING ON!!" as I watch in disbelief,

I see people jumping out of windows, 107 floors down onto the street,

56 minutes go by and the south tower ends up falling to the ground,

Thick grey smoke followed immediately and it has the weirdest sound,

Like thunder as the smoke rose at least 20 stories high,

The dark cloud chasing people around the corners of my beloved NY,

Minutes later the other tower succumbs from the damage caused by the plane,

It all seems like a movie, I don't think New York will ever really be the same,

Manhattan Island was the target for this terrorist attack,

And the Pentagon, who in their right mind has the balls to do that?

I'm up pacing back and forth now in my apartment visibly tense,

It's safe to say the war against America has officially commenced,

My girl is weighing heavily on my mind as I watch the destruction in New York,

Some kind of contact with her I need, there has to be some way we could talk,

Then I remembered about my cell phone that's still sitting in my car,

It's just downstairs so I grab my keys and left the front door ajar,

I run downstairs, unlock my car, grab the phone, and lock the car again,

Press the button to dial my inbox, hopefully to hear my girl again,

I pressed it twice, I'm so jittery and nervous, but can't help but wonder,

About my baby's flight, the size of the plane and flight number,

It still hasn't connected yet as I walk up the stairs into my place,

I don't know if it was the TV or the voice that produced that pale look on my face,

The screen switched to an anchorwoman with information on those flights,

I turn up the TV and sat down; my anxiety has now just reached new heights,

"We have information about the flight numbers of the planes that crashed,"

She started reading from a paper that she was just passed,

Then everything almost went silent, it's like I was in a pool and was hearing noises,

That echoed through my head, staring at the screen, but not the hearing voices,

I'm scared to even hear the descriptions of the planes and their destinations,

Breaking out in cold sweats getting the urge to change the station,

But I must know for sure, see I have to know more,

Meanwhile my phone is saying "To hear the current message, please press four."

The newscaster confirmed that the plane that hit tower two was from United Airlines,

From Boston to Los Angeles, and hit the building a little after nine,

I went completely numb, drop the phone, and fell back onto the couch in a horrified stupor,

Didn't know what to do, what to feel, this heinous act didn't suit her,

Tears falling down my face as I blankly stare off into space,

I can't, I can't breathe, and I wish that I were in her place,

Because my baby didn't deserve this, not now, not ever,

We were destine to grow old together, I knew this as soon as I met her,

I just couldn't grasp the reasoning behind this thoughtless act,

Why my baby gotta die? Why my girl gotta be involved in something like that?

Never in a million years would I have envisioned us living apart,

Let alone dying apart, somebody successfully just took my heart,

My phone keeps repeating "To hear the current message, please press four."

I wiped the tears off of my face and slowly pick the phone up off of the floor,

Can't stop thinking about my girl and how I'd never love another,

I press four on my keypad only to hear the sweet voice of my lover,

"Oh God I hope you get this, something has gone terribly wrong,"

"I'm calling from the phone in the bathroom, I'm afraid that I can't talk long,"

"We're getting hijacked by a couple guys with orange box cutters and knives,"

"Speaking this crazy language and talking about they're gonna start taking lives,"

"Baby I'm scared and I miss you so, I would give anything to be in your arms today,"

"Because I know that you would do whatever to keep me out of harm's way,"

"If this is the last time I talk to you, I want you to know I love you endlessly,"

"You're the very thing I wake up for, the very thing I wanted our kids to be,"

"I will always love you and with every tear that drops from my eye,"

"Are wishes that I was with you, instead of on this plane, falling from the sky"

"Oh God they're banging on the door, baby I need you to know,"

"I cherished everyday together, and all the places we would go,"

"All the things we would do and see, it was always you and me,"

"Together forever, though apart, you know you got my heart eternally,"

"I'd give it all away for just another day with you in my life,"

"I love you, you're my everything, and I'll always be your wife."

"End of message."

Late

"Wait, wait hold up, what exactly do you mean?"

Let me calm down a bit and try not to scream,

She's saying that her period's late and she don't know what to do,

I advise her to take a Clear Blue Easy, Fact Plus, hell, take two,

"Because you and I both know it wasn't supposed to go this far,"

I'm thinking back to all the freaky shit we did in my car,

She's panicking to the point that she's not even making sense,

I gotta make her calm down and face the consequence,

Of our actions of that night, this is not the time to start a fight,

Thinking out loud "My life is fucked!" oops, that didn't come out right,

Everything that I wanted to do for my life has come to a screeching halt,

Just 'cause of the result, of a one night stand, and it's my fault,

We had no protection but it felt like the time was right,

Plus, I was horny as hell, contemplating if I may, if I might,

Just do it just once, I think I could really love her,

Saying anything to convince myself that it's ok without a rubber,

She wants me to meet her because she's spazzing out,

I've been up all night, I'm about to crash out, and I'm on the road to pass out,

"Can you meet me at 4:00?" she asked whiles she's on the verge of crying,

"I can't believe this is happening, I just feel like dying,"

I try my best to try to make her think a little more clear,

She needs to calm down, she's losing it, I fear,

That she'll do something stupid, so I try to keep her on the phone,

"Who's there with you," I ask "Are you there all alone?"

"Yes, for now," she said, "But Sheila's says she's coming over,"

Damn, I hate her friend Sheila, as soon as she knows, it'll be all over,

She goes on to tell me that her family would kill her if they were to find out,

That she's pregnant and her life would be good as over no doubt,

They'll send her back to the Dominican Republic, although it's beautiful, she doesn't love it,

Her friends, her dreams, her life and future here in the states is what she covets,

Dang, I don't even know what to tell her, not just hers, but my world too will flip,

I can't be worried about this now, I'm about to go on my senior trip,

As you can see, my priorities are kinda twisted,

I'm worried about a test in 5th period French, not her period and if she missed it,

I again tell to "Cálmate, cálmate," I tell her "I'll be there in an hour,"

"I just got home from playing ball, I have to take a shower,"

She tells me that she'll still be there on her bed, crying all alone,

I'm thinking damn how am I gonna get her off this dang phone,

She tells me bye and right before I could say it back,

She tells me to pick her up a pregnancy test, preferably a 2 pack,

"Wait, hold up, hold up," I said "How come you can't go buy one,"

"You're the one who has to use it, you're the one who has to try some."

She replies, "You know my cousin works at the Walgreens up the block,"

"Do you think I'm going up there to ask for a Clear Blue Easy, I think not,"

"That's why you have to go, look, it's really not that tough,"

"Look I'm in no condition to go, I'm already dealing with enough."

"Alright, alright," I yell, "I'll go and get the damn thing,"

She told me that when I get them to go and give her a ring,

I agreed, but right before I could get off the phone,

She tells me that if her Dad finds out, it's her he's gonna disown,

Because her sister got pregnant, and she wasn't even a junior,

And with her only being a sophomore, he'll do that much sooner,

She states that she's been crying off and on for some time now,

"And all the pressure my sister had could be mine now,"

"How could I have been so stupid," she says, "Now I'm caught up in the mix,"

"My sister made me an auntie at the tender age of six,"

"My Mom got pregnant early, her sisters and Mom too,"

"It was a cycle that I told myself that I would never get locked into!"

Man she's really trippin' and I'm starting to worry too,

Because if indeed she is pregnant, what the fuck am I gonna do,

Our conversation finally ends and I jump into the shower,

I'll make it a quickie, after playing ball I usually take a ½ hour,

I get out and get dressed and start looking around my bedroom,

At any available space that I might have to fit a crib soon,

"HELL NO!" I say out loud, "There's no way that she's pregnant,"

"I see my future in chapters, and there ain't no room for this segment."

I grab my coat and keys and I head for the door,

Knowing that I don't want to do this, but I just got to be sure,

Walking to the elevator, and I'm quietly freakin' out and stressing,

I call my best homie and honestly start confessing,

"Yo, son you remember that girl Yessenia from up the block,"

"Her cousin Lisa drives that yellow souped-up I-Roc,"

"Yo man, we got it on in a real way a couple of days ago,"

"In her car no doubt, dog, believe me when I say so,"

"It was wild and crazy, but now my future's looking hazy,"

"Because she might be pregnant, and it might be my baby,"

"I'm in a tight spot and I don't know what to do,"

"I'm headed to Walgreens to get a Clear Easy Plus or Fact Blue,"

"Whatever it's called, I don't know, son I'm straight up losing it"

"How could a one night stand turn into this confusing shit?"

"I played it cool with her while she was on the phone,"

"Like it was no big thing, while she's spazzing at home all alone,"

"But Yo, I'll catch ya later, I gotta go get this damn test,"

"And hopefully put this 'I'm pregnant' stuff to rest,"

"Oh yeah, one more thing, please keep this on the low,"

"I can't afford to have ANNNNNY body else know."

We hang up and I look at what my world's coming too,

And for a brief second, I wonder what Yessenia's going through,

I've been laying in the same spot since I hung up the phone,

Anxiously waiting for the tests, while through my crazy thoughts I roam,

Through all of my dreams and future accomplishments that I wanted,

But it seems like I'm just cursed to be a young mother, dammit I'm haunted,

No more knowledge bowls or meetings with the student body,

Just looks of amazement at my protruding body,

But wait, I'm talking like I'm already pregnant, I gotta keep it straight,

But every time I think of my predicament my damn brain aches,

I can't imagine having a child and living in this place,

It's already cramped in here, where exactly would I find the space,

Where would I find the privacy to do what I got to do?

A baby and school, I don't know, I don't know if I'll make it through,

I keep replaying that night over and over in my head,

To impatient to find a room, settled for a backseat instead,

Maybe if things weren't so rushed, it would've turned out a little better,

Man, if this news gets out, you might as well brand me with the scarlet letter,

Because I'll be that girl who had a baby before she even got a work permit,

And everything that I've accomplished to this point won't be worth shit,

I'll be that girl lugging diaper bags mixed with books for school,

Lying to myself, saying that maternity clothes looks so cool,

I'm the fool, I'll admit it, and I'll take the blame because I did it,

Me making it out of high school without a child...................uh forget it,

Not to mention this guy that I'm with isn't even my ideal choice,

For baby daddy material, he doesn't even have bass in his voice,

Selfish and self-centered, Jeff's a mama's boy to the bone,

Why'd I mess around in the car, I should've taken my ass home,

"Damn this, I need to know," I yelled, taking deep breaths and getting pissy,

Put a pillow over my face and scream, "WHERE THE HELL IS HE?"

So I'm sitting outside of Walgreens in my car procrastinating,

Do I really wanna go up in there, hmm I'm debating,

Shit, let's get this over with, I'm sooo over all the drama,

Gotta start thinking of a game plan if indeed she is a mama,

"Hey great game the other night," someone yelled, "I really love your game!"

"Thanks!" I reply, knowing that my life might not be the same,

If indeed that Fact Plus shows a positive reading,

A whole bunch of smelling salts is something that I'm going to be needing,

So I walk in playing it cool, I head straight for the magazines,

My heart is beating kind of fast as I'm trying not to be seen,

I pick up a Sports Illustrated and kinda thumb through it,

Trying to conjure up the courage and the balls to go do it,

Its two aisles down and I need to get going,

At this rate, by the time I get the test, she'll already be showing,

I move a little closer to that section, but panicked and started looking at razors,

Thinking about buying one to cut my wrist if indeed it's a baby I gave her,

Jus' playin', just trying to make light of my situation,

I decided to just go get it, all these feminine products that I'm facing,

First Response, AccuClear, E.P.T, Clear Blue Easy,

Fact Plus, Equate, Walgreens brand, Clear Blue Digital, man this ain't easy,

So I grab the E.P.T because it is the error proof test,

Figuring its 99.9% sure, so it has to be the best,

So I grab the box and I'm contemplating on getting two,

But at $17.39, I think just one box will do,

Trying to play it low key, hoping the clerk doesn't know me,

She's kinda taking her time with the people that's before me,

I'm getting frustrated, my present situation, I'm starting to hate it,

That unprotected sex game has me wondering why I even played it,

The stress is building up I need to get the hell out of Walgreens,

Trying not to make eye contact, still trying to go unseen,

Damn, what is taking this chick so long to ring up this stuff?

Its cashiering 101, come on it's not even that tough,

The photo desk is open so I go over there in a hurry,

I'm stressing over nothing, it'll be negative, I ain't worried,

The cashier looks at me and then looks at the box and then shakes her head,

Mutters something under her breath, I couldn't hear what she said,

I just want her to throw it in the bag so that I can hurry up and leave,

But no she starts to pry, this is exactly what I don't need,

She tries to be slick as she's getting all into my business,

Who's this for? Is this for you? Come on man, what is this?

"I just need my stuff," I said "Can you please speed this whole thing up,"

"I got some things to do, and you're definitely holding me up."

She gives me a stank look and puts it in the bag that hastily grab,

She asks if I want the receipt, I told her keep it, she's back there all mad,

But whatever, I'm on my way to see Yessenia and officially see what's going on,

She's probably freakin' the hell out, because this has really taken too long,

I pull off in my car and I just blast my music to help ease my mind,

Man I hope she ain't pregnant I'm thinking to myself, everything's gonna be fine,

I don't know if I even believe that, this could really be an issue,

I really don't think my life should be jacked just because of a lil' miscue,

Sitting at a red light, trying to get my head right,

Me giving up everything for a baby mama, is in dead sight,

Then I get a text that kinda snaps me outta my daze,

I'm way too young to be going through a baby mama phase,

I'm on my way to Yessenia's to give her the bag of tests I bought,

Hopefully I played it off smooth because I really didn't want to get caught,

I pull up to her house and I look around because I still don't want to be seen,

I run up towards her stairs and to her window and I tap on her screen,

"What the hell are you doing?" says Yessenia, "How come you just didn't come in?"

I say "I didn't want to run in to your nosey friend or any of your kin",

She goes and opens the front door and lets me in her house,

I asked her why's she so bummy and what's with the wrinkles on her blouse,

"I've been laying down and crying all day, stupid", she said, "Wow, you sure know what to say!"

"Look," I said "Let's get this done, I ain't got too much time to play."

She looks and says "What EXACTLY do you have to do that's more important than this?"

I respond "A whole lot more than standing around watching you piss."

"Whatever, you're a dumb ass!" she says and snatches the bag and storms to the back,

I'm thinking ain't no way in hell I could spend 18 years dealing with that,

So I'm sitting on her bed and I'm thinking of my potential life with her,

And the possibilities of being a very young husband and wife with her,

Because if indeed she's preggers, her family's gonna flip out,

And with a family full of young mothers, they are definitely gonna trip out,

Because she was supposed to be the one to break that so called family curse,

And ending up pregnant by me, would only just make things worse,

Because they even don't like me and I sure as hell don't like them,

And every chance that they get, our relationship they will condemn,

Which means that she just might have to shack up with me,

And my Mom really isn't too fond of her, which makes this whole situation shaky,

She's in the bathroom with the door closed, and the faucet running,

She's trying to get the urge to go to the bathroom, but I guess it's not coming,

I might have to go in the bathroom to see exactly what's really going on,

And to help her speed up the process because it's already taking too long,

As she's looking around her bathroom, she notices the lack of space for baby stuff,

Nowhere to set a baby tub, or a bag filled with baby soaps, toys and other stuff,

She grabs the box and reads the directions over and over again,

She reads about when to do it and the procedures to begin,

She's nervous as she fiddles around with the test still in its wrapper,

She's thinking that the end result could possibly put her life in the crapper,

The urge finally comes and she's uneasy but anxious to know the results,

Of her potentially life altering moment, that could thrust them into the lives of adults,

Clumsy all of a sudden, she tries to open up the package but she can't,

She's mumbling something under her breath, and it almost sounds like a chant,

"Come on, come on, come on, come on dammit I can't get this thing out"

An easy process for some who aren't facing a future of doubt,

She finally gets it open and she drops the wrapper on the floor,

At this point in time, her boyfriend is now knocking on the door,

"Aye Yo, what's the deal, did you do it already or what?" shouts Jeff,

He continues "I know you hear me talking, stop acting like you're deaf."

She rips open the door, "WHAT!!" she says, "Why are you so loud?"

"And no you can't come in, this bathroom's too small for a crowd."

"The hell I ain't," replies Jeff "This test holds the answer for the both of us,"

"And depending on the results, it could be business as usual for most of us."

A dejected look comes across Yessenia's face, she turns around lets him in,

She's tell him to lean on the wall because she's about to begin,

She pulls down her panties and sits on the toilet holding the test,

She looks at Jeff and you can tell she's secretly hoping for the best,

She's having a hard time getting over what Jeff had said earlier with zest,

But you know what they say, a lot of truth is said in jest,

She sticks the test in her urine stream and waits about 7 seconds,

She has to wait about 5 minutes before she could even check in,

With the test, so she takes this time to ask Jeff what he meant,

With that slick little "Business as usual for most of us" comment,

"I'm just sayin'" says Jeff, "It could go back to the was,"

"No more stressing about our potential future together, mainly because,"

"It'll be like a do over, it'll be cool girl just wait for it,"

"We just might've dodged a bullet, no need for a debate on it."

She washes her hands and looks at him in the mirror,

Turns around dries her hands and towards Jeff, she moves nearer,

Yessenia looks at the test, and still no results to show,

She grabs Jeff's hand and with a smile, she says "You know,"

"I don't think it'll be that bad, you know, if it turns out to be positive,"

"The hardest thing I think would be finding a new spot to live,"

"Because, staying here with my family in an already crowded house,"

"I gotta go, but they won't let me if I do not have a spouse,"

Jeff gives Yessenia a weird look and then pulls his hand back,

He yells "This was not supposed to happen, how could you not understand that?"

"Don't start making any plans for baby Jordans and Timberlands,"

"Thinking it's all picnics in the park, with the three of us holding hands"

"You were supposed to go to college and be the first in your family to do that,"

"Now it seems that you're cool with the thought of having a child, nah screw that!"

"You need to be focused because I'm not trying to be a high school Dad,"

"And don't even start with those eyes, I could care less if you're sad,"

"Honestly, think about the life that we could afford to give a baby,"

"I have college trips coming up, and if you think I'm missing those, you're crazy."

She looks away then looks at herself in the mirror,

She says "What are you saying?" he responds "Do I have to make it any clearer?"

"Look, I don't want to seem like the bad guy, but this having a baby crap can't fly,"

"I thought we were on the same page earlier, this is not what I meant by,"

"Me and you, ride or die no matter what, no if's and's or maybes,

"I know I'm coming off like an asshole, BUT WE AIN'T READY FOR A BABY!"

Yessenia's eyes start to well up with tears but she doesn't let the fall,

She turns around, out of his view to wipe her eyes with her washcloth off the wall,

As she turns back around she see the test and stares at it,

She picks it up and shows it to Jeff and he just glares at it,

Both of their mouths, wide open, not exactly what one of them were hoping,

How do they get back to where they were yesterday, now that true feelings are in the open?

Jeff's clearly not ready for a baby and he thought Yessenia was on board,

All of his negative sentiments earlier with his girl have definitely struck a chord,

Could they move on with each other knowing exactly how words can cut?

She puts the test on the bathroom counter, turns to Jeff and says "Now what?"

One Night Out

10:00

My girls always try to get me to go out, they say I work too much,

That I need to have fun, chill and relax and get in touch,

With my free spirit, usually, I'm not really trying to hear it,

But what the hell might as well, I mean who am I to fear it?

So we make plans to go clubbing and dance the night away,

They want me to go so bad that they are even willing to pay,

They said to meet them downtown around nine; I said that's fine,

Oh, I need to see if I could get an outfit on my lunch if I have time,

12:00 pm

Damn Dillard's is so expensive, they don't even have what I crave,

Strolling around the Aurora Mall I decide to go into Rave,

The clothes there are for teenage girls with no inhibitions,

About wearing some of these outfits, could I get into that? Keep wishing,

But they do have a Tommy skirt with a matching Tommy midriff,

Tommy sling back shoes that comes with a Tommy Girl perfume gift,

12:45 pm

Then I go into Victoria's Secret for a bra and panty set,

Found what I like, slide the Visa; bag it up, time to jet,

1:00 pm

So I clock back in, with an eager adolescent grin,

I can't believe that I'm actually going out with my friends,

3:00 pm

Oh yeah, time to clock out, see you guys all on Monday,

Still trying to convince myself that I deserve to have fun at least for one day,

In the car, music pumpin', and I'm starting to feel alright,

Still excited but uneasy about going out tonight,

3:45 pm

So here I am in traffic, but I'm not stressing it too much,

I'm listening to The Nutty Professor Soundtrack, R. Kelly "Just A Touch"

4:30 pm

Make it home as I check my mail I'm saying "Damn that traffic was wild."

Let me see, bills, bills, bills got me sounding like Destiny's Child,

So I go upstairs to relax, maybe try my new outfit on,

Take a quick lil' power nap before I go get my boogie on,

7:30 pm

Damn, I over slept as I hurry into the shower,

Wash my hair, paint my nails, it all takes about an hour

8:35 pm

I grab my phones to see if my girls could pick me up,

It's ringing, it's ringing, it's ringing, "Hey wassup!"

"Are you guys gonna pick me up because I don't have any gas,"

"And besides you know where we're going so I guess we'll get there fast."

"Is it cool with you? Ok, then I'll meet you here around ten,"

"I'll be downstairs in the lobby, see you soon, alright then."

9:00 pm

Trying to do my hair, but I'm running low on hairspray,

I resort to gel and mousse hoping that'll make my hair stay,

9:45 pm

I finally get dressed and must say that I look good,

Hair and makeup looks flawless, new outfit is bangin', as it should,

Damn I look good, good enough to get some digits,

Lady's Cool Water on the neck, breast and navel, in case I meet a midget,

10:05 pm

I'm in the lobby chillin', nervous but steadily waiting,

For my girls to show up, damn, talk about procrastinating,

Here they go; they're pulling up in a Cadillac Escalade,

I guess it's something that they rented, don't want to know how much that they paid,

10:37 pm

We hit the F-Stop first and it was pretty cool,

Some guys approached us with some lines straight out high school,

Like, "Are your legs tired, because you've been running through my mind all day,"

And, "Girl you got me speechless, I don't even know what to say,"

Plus, "Ooh baby could I bother you by asking what's your sign?"

I respond, "Yes you can, it's STOP, please come back with another line,"

"Can you have my number? Only if your name is Kobe."

Where are my girls, because these guys are making want to play low key,

12:45 am

A couple hours past, some body shot and 2 cherry Cosmos later,

You'd think I owed the guy money the way I keep tipping the waiter,

My girls, both trashed, are in the corner talking to some guys,

One too many Midori Sours has my temperature on the rise,

12:30 am

I'm feeling crazy sick and am soooo ready to go,

"What!! You can't have my number, how many times I gotta say no!"

Hold up is that my song? "I'm Slim Shady, yes I'm the Real Shady!"

If this girl bump me again, it's gonna be me and you lady,

I head back from the dance floor as my girl's flag me down,

"Come to the booth with us, have a seat girl, sit down!"

Kelly introduces me to these 3 Backstreet wannabees,

"Excuse me fellas," says Kelly, "This is my girl Rylee,"

I said "Hi", but it just didn't feel right, just didn't vibe with me,

Kelly and Kim both said to play along, alright, whatever we'll see,

1:07 am

These guys are really boring and it starting to ruin my night,

On the dance floor, the girl who bumped me earlier just got into a fight,

These guys keep the drinks coming and steady paying for it all,

I'm so twisted, that if I stand up, I just know that I'm going to fall,

So I ask Kim to come with me to the bathroom so that I could freshen up,

Kelly tells the guys that "We'll be back, so don't go messing up,"

"The chances of getting," and I'm thinking that this bitch is trippin',

No she didn't promise these guys some sex, she needs an ass whippin',

1:15 am

We get into the bathroom and I go off, "Hey Kelly, what the hell was that?"

"Why you promise those dudes some sex, that was soooo wack,"

She explained to me that it's just a game that she plays,

In order for those drinks to keep flowing, somebody gotta pay,

I'm so disgusted that I didn't even touch up my make-up,

"I tell ya this," I said "Tell them wassup, or this lil' party, I'm about to break up!"

1:35 am

I'm heated now as I storm back over to the booth,

I broke it down for the guys, not waiting on Kelly to tell the truth,

I say "Regardless of what she said, it ain't that type of party,"

"I'm going home by myself, in other words, with NOBODY"

"Excuse me," I said as I go back to the bathroom to get them,

I barge in the door and I find them whispering, I interrupt "All right listen,"

"I really don't know exactly what the two of you had planned,"

"But I ain't sleeping with those dudes because none of them are my man,"

1:49 am

They apologize and we hug it out and return to see 3 drinks waiting

Kelly and Kim both downed theirs, damn lushes, but I'm still debating,

I take a sip and look at it, Kim calls me prude and to stop procrastinating,

I state "Since when does a Pina Colada have a salty after taste? I'm just sayin'"

1:55 am

The ugly lights come on and I'm headed towards the door,

My girls are still with those guys, but I ain't checking for them no more,

So I'm leaning on the Escalade, just dizzy and not feeling right,

I guess those couple of sips of that Pina Colada might've done me in for the night,

Just taking deep breaths of the night air, I'm so ready to go home,

Ready to start hugging that cold white porcelain throne,

Now here comes my girls, feet stumbling, purse fumbling,

My respect for them, crumbling. Incoherent words they're mumbling,

But a couple words that they said I was able to make out,

Like we're going something back to something or someone's house,

2:00 am

"Back to whose house," I yell, "Ain't nobody here my spouse,"

"The only house I'm interested in going to is The Waffle House,"

"Or the International House of Pancakes, I could say your plan flaked,"

"Because right about now is the very end of this date!"

Then one dude says, "Hey Kelly, would you please calm ya girl down,"

"Let her know I got a cool little spot 20 minutes outta town."

"Look," I started to tell him, "I don't know you from the next man,"

"So me going to your house, nope, better think of your next plan,"

"Come ahnn!" slurred Kelly with her drunk stare, "It'll be ok,"

"A ½ hour at the most, ok, then we'll be on our way,"

"Come on, do this one for us Rye, we never get to do stuff,"

"He lives out in Cherry Hills; come on this decision ain't that tough."

Damn, my loyalty to my friends has me doing things that I don't do,

And sleeping with these guys is definitely something that I won't do,

Two of the guys jump in a black 600 Mercedes Benz,

While the third guy drives the SUV that I arrived in with my friends,

One of the guys say, "Come on ladies." as they stumble to the Mercedes,

I turn to the third guy and advise him not to get all shady,

So we follow this damn speed demon out to high society,

Damn these houses are nice, but why is this dude keep eyeing me,

I keep getting to the point where I feel like I want to black out,

I pull down the visor for the vanity mirror, damn I looked so cracked out,

All of these twists and turns at high speeds has me feeling queasy,

The more I thought about the house, the more I felt uneasy,

I'm finding it so hard to hold on to any single thought,

And I'm wondering if there was something inside the drinks that they had bought,

Damn I can't think straight, did they do it? Hold up, wait,

My damn head is hurting so bad that I can't even see straight,

We were there for all the drinks, the Jack and Cokes, the Midori Sours,

We were there for all of them except for the Coladas that they said that were ours,

I'm zoning out, but I'm trying my best to stay alert,

He thinks he's funny; his damn seat warmer is burning my ass through this skirt,

2:37 am

Anyway, we get to their spot and I gotta say that it's really nice,

My girlfriends were already starting to pour the Moet Chandon that they had on ice,

The hot tub, the sauna, go in? Nah, I don't wanna,

They said that I'm being a drag and to go sit myself in the corner,

"That's fine with me!" I said as the girls continue drinking heavily,

All I want are my goose down pillows and a cozy spot where my head should be,

3:07 am

So I'm sitting in the corner and I must say this house is tight,

Eyes are even more blurry from the incandescent and florescent lights,

Neon strips on the floors that lead to oversized doors,

Black lacquer coffee tables, champagne glasses by the scores,

From the looks of things, I can say that these guys like to party,

I try to flag down that one guy; um, I think his name is Marty,

"Hey, yeah um excuse me, could I get some Tylenol, Advil or Aleve,"

"You know, something so that this pain in my head I could relieve?"

I'm being a smart ass, but my head is really killing me,

With my current attitude and slick mouth, I could tell he wasn't feelin' me,

The three guys look at each other and someone said it was in the cabinet,

Told Marty he'd have to look around, he's not even sure that he has it,

My girls are getting super friendly, if you know what I mean,

Just buggin' over the fact that they have their own tanning machine,

Next to the pool, as Kelly strips down to her undies,

Yelling "I'll be in the pool in case anybody wants me!"

3:15 am

I'm feeling a little better now, as I feel the breeze from the patio,

Kinda just clearing my head, as one of the guys decide to go,

With Kelly to the pool and the other with Kim in the sauna,

She wants me to join them, but I told her I wasn't gonna,

I'm thinking, these little hoe bags left me here all alone,

Thinking that I cannot wait to get my drunk self home,

Finally I get some pain pills from the dude I sent to get some,

He said it wasn't Tylenol, but stronger, go ahead and try one,

"What is it?" I asked before I opened my mouth and stuck it,

But the mixture of lights and the pain, ahh fuck it,

3:57 am

He said he wanted me to sit next to him and watch some TV,

I told him alright, but that he's gonna have to come and help me,

With one arm over his shoulder he helps me over to the couch,

I'm too out of it to sit up straight, so I'm sitting kinda slouched,

He has this big ass 80" HDTV,

He wants to know what I want to watch, and I told him it doesn't even matter to me,

He puts in the DVD of the movie Don't Say a Word,

I told him "No funny stuff" and he responded "You have my word"

4:15 am

By midway through the beginning I start to hear moaning from the back,

I can't believe these girls, don't even know how to act,

Totally embarrassed by my friends, and I know he feels the same,

Then I take notice to the fact that I'm not feeling any pain,

4:21 am

No headache, no blurry eyes, damn these pills are great,

But it's hard for me to move, what? Hold up wait,

I asked him sternly, "What's the name of those damn pills?"

He replies "Don't say nothing, just lay there and be still,"

Hell no I thought, "WHAT!" I yell as he leans over to try to kiss me,

He misses me; I managed to turn my head quite swiftly,

It's like I got very little to jerky movement in my arms and legs,

I start to cry "Please don't do this. STOP!! Please I beg!!

4:38 am

It all seemed to happen so quick, the movie, the moaning and then bam,

Then all of a sudden I realize just where the hell I am,

He turns up the sound on the TV to try to mask my cries,

I guess he didn't want to bring any attention from his guys,

I know what he's doing and what's being done, oh shit,

He yanks down my skirt and up the seam, a big slit,

I'm kicking and I'm screaming, he covers my mouth as he's leaning,

All of his weight on his hand, on my lips, I'm not believing,

4:43 am

This is happening to me, why is this happening to me?

With my last little bit of control, to his nuts, I force my knee,

He gave a lil' bit but not enough to get away,

Because the full effect of the drug has me unable to get away,

He's playing a dangerous game that I don't even want to play,

The stitching on my panties, oh God I hope it stays,

4:47 am

But it doesn't, now I'm giving him all that I could muster up,

He's cutting off my air supply, my face is starting to fluster up,

4:51 am

I'm starting to see white stars and everything that goes along with that

I'm starting to feel faint, then everything just fades to black,

4:52 am

4:53 am

4:54 am

4:55 am

4:56 am

4:57 am

4: 58 am

4:59 am

5:00 am

5:01 am

I start to come to a little bit because this guy's being so damn rough,

I feel like I'm paralyzed and in no position to even act like I'm tough,

He moved me to some bedroom and shut the door behind him,

He takes off his shirt and I'm laying there deciding,

Should I just lie here and let this asshole continue to have his way,

And feel like shit tomorrow, next week, forever and a day?

"Hell No!" I think as he manages to tear off my blouse,

My screams are becoming desperate cries to anyone that's in the house

5:05 am

He slaps me a couple of times and I try to grab his hair,

Then he stops and gives me the coldest and sickest stare,

5:09 am

Somehow I get control of my arms and legs and he has a look of surprise

When I was able to cock back and punch him right in his eye,

5:13 am

I start fighting, scratching anything I could touch, kicking, biting,

I cannot get him off and just then my fear is severely heightened,

As he puts one hand around my throat and the other undoes his belt,

Please Lord no, I thought; it's going to happen now I felt,

This sudden sense of urgency as he tries to enter me,

HIs left leg is on my thigh, and as for kicking, he's preventing me,

5:17 am

My other leg is hoisted up and locked inside his arm,

I gotta do something now to try to prevent any further harm,

I'm starting to feel dizzy and nauseous all over again,

I guess the fighting shook up everything I had in my stomach and then,

5:21 am

He did it, oh God he did it and with every slow thrust,

With every slow moan, I felt my world slowly crush,

I can't stop the tears from streaming down my bruised face,

All I wanted to do is get up and get the hell up out of that place,

I pleaded with him, "Please stop, no, GET THE FUCK OFF ME!"

I gave him one last burst of energy to try to get him off me,

Then I conceded, I could no longer conjure up the strength to fight,

I tried to hold my tears; I tried and tried with all my might,

But I couldn't, I just laid there, dead, I just laid still,

Too numb to move from him taking me against my will,

For every drive into my unwilling body, I release a higher cry,

It's like I gave up on my life, I'm just lying there waiting to die,

I just want him to stop so that I can gather the splinters of my life he's shattered,

Then I start thinking about condoms and how to him it didn't even matter,

5:27 am

He's done now, done destroying everything that I've built up for years,

All my self-confidence and independence melted away like tears,

I came too far to restart my life back at square one,

On the edge of the bed having mixed emotions, deciding should I stay or run,

Cry, yell or fight, infinite rage is clouding my sight,

Feel like I've died but lived to see it all in one night,

5:35 am

I manage to get up, still crying silently, but I gather up my things,

He didn't mean to do it is the song that he sings,

"Please don't tell the cops," he said "Please I'll give you money."

I release a subdued surprise chuckle, and then he yells "This ain't funny!"

5:40 am

I explode "You slip me some shit and you think that it's all good?"

 "Drug me up, rape me on the couch and think that I should,"

"Not tell the cops and perhaps try to work this out,"

"Are you out your fuckin' mind? Do you know what this is about?"

Right now I'm screaming at the top of my lungs,

I must've blacked out, as I wobbled up to his face and swung,

So here I am, consumed by a murderous rage,

Completely wildin' out like a beast out its cage,

I shout, "It's all now, the whole shit, it was staged,"

"Plant some shit in my drink, just so you can get laid!"

I stop swinging, grab the keys to Cadillac, stumbled to the door and left,

6:03 am

Speeding and swerving through the streets and I could hardly catch my breath,

Steady having flashbacks as I speed through all these stop signs,

Thinking, "Did I lead him on? Did I show him any stop signs?"

I must stop crying, and slow down because I'm flying,

Down this one way going 60 miles an hour, and it's rising,

My cell keeps ringing off the hook, and I look,

At the ID, and its Kelly's number and that's pretty much all it took,

6:16 am

To start flipping out again, start trippin' out again, rehashing,

Everything that I've could've done, on this pedal I was mashing,

I finally pull over to contemplate my next move,

Parked the car, cracked the sunroof and the warm rays just soothe,

My tear soaked cheeks, my voice too hoarse to speak,

To psyche myself up to get the medical attention that I seek,

Or should I go home and just wallow in myself pity,

Knowing I didn't cause the events that made me feel so shitty,

6:28 am

So I drive to the hospital, feeling helpless and ashamed,

Embarrassed to the point that I don't even want to give the cops my real name,

Filling out paperwork paper work as the nurse and I wait for the cops,

Streaming images in my head, damn, I wish that it would stop,

7:24 am

As I change from my ripped clothes to a blue and white smock,

Massive blood and urine work, I'm giving them all that I got,

Questions coming from all angles, from the cops to the nurses,

I'm trying to keep my composure, but then here comes the curses,

"Why all fuckin' asking me all these questions, like somehow I wanted all of this,"

"Check the urine samples; it has to be all in the piss,"

"This motherfucker slipped something in my drink, so I think,"

"Yall are making me feel like I wanted this, you're pushing me to the brink!"

I rest my head in my hands and tell the rest of my story,

To this asshole cop who seems to only want more, he,

Wants to know his name, his address and I tell him that I'm still kinda doped up,

Any good leads you get from me are going to be slim, so don't get your hopes up,

8:00 am

The nurses excuse the cop from the room as they prepare the rape kit,

I mean the sexual assault forensic evidence in short the (SAFE) kit,

They sit me on a white sheet with combs and glass slides and labels,

Bags for my clothes and envelopes all just sitting on this table,

They grab the long cotton swabs and other stuff for a semen sample

Then go on to tell me how I'm not like the average example,

Of a rape victim because most of them go home and take a shower,

Making it harder for us to get any samples from the coward,

"Yeah, I'm not the typical victim." I said but, really I don't care,

As they place my feet in these cold stirrups four feet up in the air,

They found traces of Rohypnol in my urine and my blood,

His skin under my fingernails along with his hair and other crud,

The doctor comes in and explains all about this date rape drug,

How it impairs just about everything and leaves you with the amnesia bug,

He asked was I agitated and I responded "HELL YES!"

"We were going blow for blow, but of me, he got the best!"

They test for everything, STD's and other things I've could have contracted,

Still blaming myself for the way that he acted,

11:36 am

Hours go by and they advise me to talk to a rape counselor,

Maybe sit on today's meeting, but I ain't gonna bounce with her,

She tells me about the group sessions with women just like me,

And for me to hold it all in would be so unhealthy,

I tried to convince her that I was fine, but I am dying inside,

That little place within that I had for myself I could no longer reside,

11:49 am

We keep talking as the doctor walks in with his metal chart and pen,

He said that Marty hit me with a mixture of drugs and that's what did me in,

He said that it would be awhile before all the tests come back,

That I could leave if I want, and that they'll call me with the facts,

I continue to give more info to the cops, well, all that I could remember,

He's still acting like an ass, with remarks that's as cold as December,

He asked about my friends and how it seemed so planned,

Almost on cue Kelly and Kim burst in, both of them holding hands,

They both start crying, "Oh J, we're so sorry,"

"We had no idea that it was gonna be that type of party!"

Now they are giving their descriptions and possible addresses to that house,

While I'm behind the curtain, looking at a bag that has what remains of my blouse,

12:30 pm

My clothes are all torn and bloodied and I would really love a sweatshirt,

And some sweatpants because this hospital gown just won't work,

I'm still answering questions, but this time to a female detective,

I was so over the other guy, she's the one I would've selected,

She brings me extra clothes and shoes and we begin talking,

She asked if I was alright to walk, I said yes, so we began walking,

I ask her who in their right mind would even think to do this,

Rape and abuse a woman, and leave me with all of these damn bruises,

I tell her, "I still see his face; I still smell the stink of his breath,"

"Still feel the sweat on his skin, ohhh he needs to see death!"

I give her a fake smile but she tells me to stay strong,

For the one who did this won't be a free man for long,

We walk back to the examination room and the male cop is saying, "Are you certain,"

He repeats, "About 6'2 eyes greenish brown blue,"

"Between 180 and 235 pounds, ladies, this isn't gonna do."

As he keeps on talking, I'm only thinking about sleep,

Just to go home, take a shower, and in my bed.......creep,

I get my discharge papers and proceed to sign myself out,

Barney Fife said that he'd call me if anything he finds out,

1:23 pm

The nurse tells me to set an appointment in the next couple of days,

Like, I hear her talking, but I'm still kinda in a daze,

As we leave the hospital, I see the female detective filling out some papers,

I walk over to her and grab her hand; I just had to thank her,

"Thank you so much for helping me through this,"

"I swear if it wasn't for you, I'd doubt that I'd be able to do this,"

She gives me a hug, and tells me to go home and get some rest,

Her fellow detectives have enough leads to do the rest,

Outside the hospital surrounded by my girls, but still feel alone,

Kelly drives the Escalade and Kim takes me on home,

I put my feet on the seat and just begin to hug my knees,

Roll down the window to feel the cool afternoon breeze,

Kim just keeps talking and talking and man, I wish I was alone,

2:10 pm

We get to my building and she helps me up the stairs,

Kim goes on about getting these guys but I really don't even care,

I'm putting up a front for my friends, "See yall, I'm alright,"

"Besides, you know, it was a pretty decent night."

They both gave me hugs and heavy tears as they departed,

I tried to subdue them, but I couldn't stop what they started,

2:23 pm

I shut the door and locked it, and went to turn on the shower,

Just reflecting as I try my hardest to wash off the touch of that coward,

I scrub and I scrub, but I still feel him all on me,

No matter how much soap I use, I'll always feel him on me,

With my back against the shower wall, I slide down and cry in pain,

Wishing my pain would act like my tears and just run down the drain,

Water hitting me in the head, steady wishing I was dead,

Days to months following that night, I barely found the strength to get out of bed,

That was 4 years ago and I still suffer to this day

Can't keep a good relationship, don't like being touched in that way,

Don't like clubs, I don't do drinks, my new best friend is the Bible,

Hopefully, to lead a better life is what this is a guide to,

Now the guys that I meet, I see them in a different light,

I used to love Cool Water, not anymore, that's what he wore on that night,

Even though he's prosecuted and in jail doing big time,

The everyday struggles he faces can't compare to some of mine,

It was hard for me to walk to the podium and give you my heart,

My fears and complications of life, how should I start?

I know you'll understand, as you too also have the sight,

And live with the reality of your life changing in one night,

I feel better today, as the self-pity that's usually on me, today isn't draped,

Hi, my name is Rylee…………………………………and I've been raped.

Untitled

The person in this story is giving her eyewitness account about the event of that night. This is her deposition:

She said she wouldn't do it again, that's what she told him,

Eyes all swollen, bruised left arm she's holdin',

Looks like it's gonna need a little more than ice,

More than twice he told you not to question him or his life,

Now she's crying on the floor next to the end table,

While he's rantin' and raving, emotionally he's unstable,

Throwing things against the wall yelling "Don't worry about my whereabouts!"

She's thinking damn this is someone that I used to care about,

Her left arm's falling asleep and she's wishing that she were,

So she doesn't have to be around to see what else is to occur,

He turns around and glares "Aye, where's my damn food?"

She tries to answer him carefully without coming across rude,

So she responds, voice shaking, "It's in the oven, I didn't want it to get cold"

"The vegetables and everything else is on the stove"

The alcohol from his breath is stinking and then she gets to thinking,

About the pain in her left eye as the distance between her eyelids are shrinking,

She sees the front door and thinks that she could make a run for it,

But that current state of her body tells her she's not the one for it,

She doesn't deserve this I keep telling myself,

I always told her sticking with this man is seriously bad for her health,

He's been in the kitchen for a little over a minute,

I've had many thoughts of a box with him lying in it,

He storms out of the kitchen "Bitch, what tryin' to pull?"

"You know damn well that I like melted butter on my vegetables!"

He throws the pot of corn at her, but it misses and hits the wall,

She grabs the phone and 911 is the number she tries to call,

She unlocks it- he's coming; she presses 9 and starts running,

To the bedroom she presses 1 and thinks where the hell is the gun and,

The ammo, too late her grabs her black and blue arm,

She tries to scream out her loudest, it's the neighbors she tries to alarm,

He picks her up and slams her on the water bed with such a force,

That all the air rapidly leaves her lungs as she still fights to get him off,

Kicking and screaming, she scratches his face, he starts bleeding,

Looking around for the gun thinking that's exactly what you're needing,

She starts having flashbacks of the times he used to hold her,

Rub her back, massage her feet, but all he does now is just scold her,

She hears her friend's voice in her head saying "Girl you should leave him!"

"So what if he said he wouldn't do it again, you know you can't believe him!"

She's thinking of this, and she's thinking of that,

Between all of her thinking she continues to get smacked,

"Why you make me do this?" he says, "You know I love you baby",

He looks at the mirror on the headboard, "You know I love you baby",

His reflection from the mirror stops him from the slapping,

He gets off the bed screaming "Look how you got me acting!"

His back is towards her now, while she lies still on the bed,

Blood streaming down her face, pain ringing through her head,

She's trying not to pass out hoping the pain won't act like a sedative,

On the bed half dead, trying not to lose the will to live,

I really don't know why he was trippin', she would've gave her life for him,

If something doesn't happen soon, her life just might end tonight with him,

Many times she forgave him for countless nights of misbehaving,

STD's to her he gave and she always said that that was just his way and,

Methods to show he loves her, or whatever he likes to call it,

She's been told but is blind to the fact that he's an abusive alcoholic,

He has her on the bed sprawled out; her voice is too hoarse to call out,

She can't walk; she can't crawl, so off the bed she falls out,

She tries her hardest to stand up and make her way to the bathroom,

She tries to hurry because the condition of her body would have her collapse soon,

But she does make it in and locks the door, he yells out "Come out you whore",

"Stupid bitch, I swear, I promise I won't hit you anymore!"

Yeah, real honest right? Picture that with a Kodak,

He says "Fuck it, when I get back you better be out, where my coat at?"

"And the keys to my Ford", he finds them then walks out and slams the door,

Starts up his truck and peels off, this window of freedom she cannot ignore,

She stands up and supporting all of her weight is the bathroom sink,

The mirror reflects her bruised and battered face and she starts to think,

How much more can she take, how many "No's" lead to rape?

How much more abuse her, her mind, body and soul take,

How many doctors are gonna go against her wishes and request a rape kit,

How many times is she gonna put him in jail, then go bail him out........SHIT,

Oops I'm sorry but I've told her that "This life isn't meant for you",

"It's the same result bruised, beaten, bloodied black and blue",

She opened the bathroom door and limps her way to the kitchen,

Puts on a strong face, but silently signals me to remain hidden,

She starts to remake his plate of food, but she's slow, and it's so hard to look,

How hard she tries to keep tears from falling into the food she cooks,

The blood on her face begins to clot now as she feverishly continues cooking,

If she had a full length mirror, she could see how this man has her looking,

Time passes and she hears the F-150 as she tries to finish swiftly,

He stumbles in the door, more drunk, more pissy,

Unbalanced, speech slurred he yells "Bitch whatcha tryin' ta cook?"

Swaying side to side with that familiar evil, drunken look,

She tries to ignore him but it's obvious that she's had enough,

He's done everything short of killing her, now it's time to get tough,

She says "I remade dinner and I hope it's to your liking"

"Please" she pleads, "Please sit down and watch the Minnesota Vikings,"

"Play Dallas, it's Monday night, please honey I don't want to fight,"

"I hope the butter's melted on your corn and rice just the way you like,"

He responds "Whatever!" as he drops onto the couch,

Not even sitting up straight, he kinda has a slouch,

"Where's your mouthy daughter?" He asks, she replies "At a sleep over."

"Good," he says, "One less bitch to get even more upset over.'

She puts the food down on the coffee table and then limps back to the bathroom sink,

She takes one last look at her face in the mirror, which has now pushed her to the brink,

I'm in the coat closet, and I can see and hear it all,

There's not that much room in there, it's a good thing that I'm small,

Mom shoved me in there and told me to be quiet and don't come out,

That she'll come get me when everything is sorted out,

I'm kinda use being in here; she always says it's for my safety,

She doesn't want me to see him when gets to acting crazy,

But she comes out and changes the channel with the remote,

Now dressed in a flannel robe, she tries to talk, but her throat,

Is still hoarse but she knows exactly what it is she has to do,

He yells out "Bitch" and she quickly responds "Fuck You!"

His eyes stare wide as he wobbles up to a rise,

He starts to talk but she cuts him off "You know I despise"

"Everything you've done to me, emotional and physical scars,"

"All the disease you've brought me, all the man that you are,"

He cuts her off, yelling slurred words "What choo say ta mees?"

He's talking under his breath as he rambles off hastily,

"I know fer sures yous dun lost yer mind,"

"Talking to mees that way, I think you oughta go finds,"

"Where yous leff it at", she yells out "I've had enough,"

"What, beatin' up your wife after work makes you tough?"

"I cook for you, clean for you, when you're too drunk, even bathe your ass,"

"You're a bitch that's going to hell and ain't nothing gonna save your ass,"

"I have no life, I have no friends, I have nothing all due to you,"

"I'm at the point where I could really give a fuck about you,"

"No more bloody lips and late night trips to the O.R.,"

"No more being out for lunch and worried about seeing your car,"

"No more feeling stupid when I'm explaining bruises to my kid,"

"No more avoiding questions from my family or explaining what you did,"

"No more getting slammed in the car door, playing second to your whore,"

"No more crying on the floor, motherfucker I said NO MORE!!"

He starts charging toward her as she reaches into her robe pocket,

Pulls out the black Desert Eagle flips the safety off and cocks it,

She told me for the first time in a long time, she now has the power,

She's shaky with the gun and now it's him, who begins to cower,

She's dead silent as the tears roll down her face, now she's crying,

She tells him that there isn't much between them that's not keeping him from dying,

He walks her and she says "Please don't make me do this,"

"I don't wanna kill you baby, maybe, we could try to work through this!"

Her hand is shaking really bad now, like she couldn't hold anymore,

She flinches when he picks up his plate and throws it through the patio door,

That plate shatters the glass as it splinters everywhere,

By now I'm sure our neighbors above and below us are aware,

But they should be used to it they don't know how she goes through it,

He threatened them too, so call the cops? They won't EVEN do it,

Her friend from upstairs knocks on the door to see if she's alright,

She turns towards the door, he grabs her arm and the gun fires once into the night,

She screams as he twists her now red and purple arm,

He rips the gun outta her hand and is intent to do her harm,

He punches her in the chest so she could scream no more,

Goes to the neighbor, who by now is pounding on the door,

He opens the door, grabs the guys shirt and put the gun in the neighbors face,

My neighbor fights back but he ends up getting shot in the waist,

The shot was loud, I got startled and slightly cracked open the door,

Just in time to see my mother rise up off the floor,

She leaps onto his back, trying her hardest to choke him,

He gets her off and throws her through the patio door that is broken,

The broken glass cuts her feet really bad and now there's blood everywhere,

Her high pitched scream is for sure to carry well through the cold night air,

He follows her out there and picks her up by the throat,

Leaning her over the balcony and now her yells hit a scary note,

"So yous gonna kill me huh bitch, come on do it slut!"

He has her off of the ground by her neck so then she kicks him in the nuts,

The gun flies back into the living room as they both drop, gasping for air,

I can hear faint sirens in the distance getting near,

He again snatches her by the neck as he tries to throw her off the balcony,

I started to cry and closed my eyes and tried my hardest not to see,

He hears the cops, so he puts down my Mom and runs over to lock the door,

Puts the chain on and then gets back to what he was doing before,

Grabs my Mom by her hair and lifts her way up in the air,

And says that he's gonna throw her on the spiked fence downstairs,

He drops my mom, but struggles only to get a better grip on her,

Everything was happening so fast, it all seemed like a blur,

I felt that I had to do something, he's gonna kill my Mom for sure,

I opened the closet and tried my hardest to find that gun that fell on the floor,

I picked it up, it was soooo heavy and I can't really keep it steady,

I ran toward the patio, stood up straight, very scared but ready,

To try to save my Mom, who at this point is very weak,

No more fighting, no more screaming, she could hardly even speak,

"Dad," I yelled, my voice shaking, "I want you to stop!"

He turns around stunned, wondering if that's the gun that he had dropped,

It all happen so fast, but then again, it seemed like forever,

I remember yelling at him that "We were supposed to stay together,"

"I'm tired of her crying and her saying that you're lying,"

"I'm tired of hearing that you'd change knowing that you weren't even trying,"

"You're my Dad and I love you, but you're just an evil old man,"

"Stop hurting her please, just let go of her hand!"

As I said that the cops almost bust in,

I heard them say to get the ram because nothing else was working,

"PUT DOWN THE GUN!" he yelled as he dropped my Mom to the ground,

I told him "We want you to leave, go, we don't want you around!"

"I want you to leave and this time, leave for good!"

I swear to you that I held that gun for as long as I could,

I lowered the gun, and Mom crawled in, bleeding everywhere,

He yells "Fuck that!" and picks her up by her bloody blonde hair,

"If I die, you die bitch," he tells her, "Till death do us part!"

He throws her over, the cops bust in, and startled, I squeezed and put one through his heart,

The cops said that I flew back like four feet from the recoil, as he lay on the patio dead,

They also informed me that they heard every word that was said,

They found my Mom two stories down, alive, but legs and ribs broken pretty bad,

As I see the cops get the bag ready, I couldn't help but feel sad,

"I loved you so much," I told him "You were supposed to be mine to own in this world,"

I kissed him on the cheek and said, "I love you and will always be daddy's little girl."

Black & Gold BMX

When I was young I got a BMX bike for Christmas,

I'd be lying to you if I told you that that wasn't on my wish list,

It was black with shiny gold rims, a gold chain and patent leather black seat,

Gold handlebars, gold spokes, man this bike could not be beat,

In any neighborhood race I had, I tell ya this bike was bad,

I remember walking to the gas station to air up the tires with my Dad,

He talked about being safe and not to let anyone ride it,

And to stay in the park, but I was too excited,

To fully listen because I finally have my own bike to ride,

And it didn't snow that Christmas, so it didn't have to stay inside,

As soon as he filled up my tires I was on it pedaling away,

I could only go but so far, my Dad didn't want me to stray,

Too far ahead so I practiced doing bunny hops instead,

Getting used to the hand brakes and falling, scuffing up my Pro Keds,

As soon as I got home I parked the bike outside,

Ran inside to sweep the hallway where my bike would reside,

My family owned an upholstery shop, and we lived upstairs on top of it,

And being that it was a family shop, I had to be there, there was no stopping it,

I made sure there wasn't anything on the floor, no staples or nails,

When I think back on it, I treated my bike like it was so frail,

I sat on my stairs just at looking at my bike thinking about next spring,

How I'm going to have the hottest bike in my neighborhood and things,

Like that just made me smile, I was the happiest child,

Not knowing that the new freedom to venture off would make me wild,

Spring comes about and the weatherman officially says that winter's over,

I couldn't wait to get home from school, no time to play Red Rover,

Or kickball or dodge ball or even kick the can,

I had to go dust off my ride and show my boys that I'm the man,

I ran upstairs as fast as I could, those 20 steps felt like 10,

Changed out if my school clothes asked if I could go outside and then,

It was on!! I backed my bike out of my hallway onto the sidewalk,

I was so geeked about showing off my new bike I couldn't even talk,

I slammed the door, hopped on my bike and I was in the wind,

It all felt like slow motion and I couldn't help but grin,

As I passed my family's shop I looked inside to see who could see me,

I heard "Go 'head!!" And my Dads laugh, I was sooo cheesey,

I stopped at Pizza Heaven to go and talk to Angelo,

I was bragging all winter on my bike to him so I stopped so,

That he could see what I was talking about and see I wasn't lying,

I showed him the gold brake cables and still he was trying,

To down play my bike, he said "Ahhh it's alright,"

"Try not to mess it up, ok?" I said ok and took flight,

Across the street into the park and I coasted onto the ball court,

You couldn't tell me I wasn't fresh, well at least that's what I thought,

I felt like a star, like Michael Knight and his K.I.T.T car,

Being adventurous left me with a couple of trick scars,

One day I leaned my bike on the fence so that I can watch it while I played ball,

While still keeping my head on a swivel, listening for my Dads call,

There was this one kid named Shawn, but we called him Marble Man,

Because rumor has it that he can fit 2 marbles in his nostrils and,

He had a bike too so of course we had to race,

Me on my new bike, I wasn't trying to come in second place,

A little kid named Vance set up the route for us to race,

Around that time, more kids gathered around to see what was taking place,

He said we had to start from the slides and head out of gate,

Down Tuckahoe Road past Crock's corner store and Louie Liquors to Altonwood Place,

Follow that block all the way to Dunbar and make a right,

Onto Runyon Avenue and haul ass up the street on your bikes,

I was a little nervous because I never been down Altonwood,

So I didn't know about the street and if the path was all good,

Cracks in the pavement, dogs, trash cans, it's all new to me,

But now all the neighborhood kids that were out came over to see,

So I get on my bike and I look at Marble Man and smile,

"You know I'm gonna win," I said "Because losing ain't my style."

He tell me to get ready to because he's going to win,

Vance said "Everybody to the slides, it about to begin!"

I was nervous because it was to be my first race,

And like I told Shawn, I wasn't trying to be in second place,

Everybody chimed in "ON YOUR MARK, GET SET, GO!"

And we both took off, neither one of us was slow,

Shawn got out the park first and started going down the street,

I was right on his heels, he wasn't going to be easy to beat,

He's on the sidewalk and he flies past the store and to the first turn,

He knows this route, this is something that I'll later learn,

I'm right behind him, but then someone comes out of the front door,

Of Louie Liquors which causes me to slow down and fall behind even more,

But I kicked it back in gear and I'm making up the space,

Between the two of us, yes see, now this has become a race,

I passed this house and seen a cute light skinned girl outside and it made me take notice,

Of her location I wanted to be the only one who knows this,

The sidewalk was all choppy, loose concrete and stuff,

So I bunny hop into the street and it wasn't that tough my,

I'm pretty close to him and he sees me and he turns on Dunbar,

By the time I get to Dunbar he's on Runyon Ave, and he's far,

Ahead of me so I start really going in, pedaling my ass off,

It was like the space shuttle, right after someone says blast off,

I stayed on the sidewalk but the low tree branches caused some problems,

So I decided to get in the street hoping that would kinda solve them,

One of the slates of concrete was broken and pointing up, kinda like a ramp,

I took that as a sign and on this race I just had placed my stamp,

I hit that concrete and caught crazy air, it was scary,

I screamed out "YEAH BOY!" hoping that Marble Man would hear me,

He looked back and seen me and really started going faster,

It didn't even matter, I was out to show the park that I was the master,

The rhythmic sound of my tires on the pavement made for a perfect soundtrack,

Of this epic bike race, oh snap a pothole, I gotta get around that,

No time to swerve so I bunny hopped and heard ooh's and ahhs from the park kids,

Who were watching from the finish line, kids with no bikes, that's what they all did,

Now we're neck and neck and I'm easily pulling away,

I'm steady cheezin' as I'm tasting victory I hear somebody say,

DANNY!! Oh snap, that was my Dad calling me from the back door of our shop,

Which, as luck would have it, could see all the way down the block,

As I crossed the finish line I was getting high fives and praise from all of the kids,

But as quick as I was enjoying this, it all came to a skid,

"Come here!" Said my father and nobody want to hear that, especially in public,

I got grounded and me and my BMX got separated again but that just made me love it,

More, I remember walking past it every day to go to school or the corner store,

To go play ball or to hang with friends outside in the park or,

When I had to work in the shop my desire to ride it wouldn't stop,

When I done with being grounded, I was back on the block,

I was grounded the whole spring, due to bad grades and stuff,

Being grounded was kinda easy, not having my bike was tough,

It was summer time now and let me tell you how Runyon Heights Park worked,

There were arts and crafts for the kids, lunch, kind of like daycare while the parents worked,

There were adults that helped out and that kept us all I n line,

And if you disrespected them in any way, they'll tell your parents in no time,

Most of the kids took part in the parks arts and crafts,

Some of the kids were related to most of the staff,

I remember one day going to the park to play some ball,

"Hey, Danny come here!" one of my friends had called,

I looked up and I saw the same girl I seen when I raced Marble Man,

This was the first time I've seen her out and it ruined my plan,

I wanted to get at her first before anyone else had the chance,

So I went up to my man and got introduced in my B Boy stance,

He said, "Keisha this is Danny, Danny this is Keisha,"

My heart started beating super loud, like it was plug into some speakers,

She said "Hi" and I responded with a "Wassup",

I guess my days of being cool around girls were pretty much up,

The girls took her over near the swings and I couldn't stop staring,

At this girl, in the background I could hear all the guys daring,

Each other to see who's going to be the one to sit with her at lunch,

I just wanted to play ball, no more conversing with this bunch,

I walk on to the court and started to just shoot around,

Basketball was my first love, I just loved hearing that sound,

Of the ball hitting the pavement and the swish from a jump shot,

Playing shirts vs. skins because it's summer time, it'll get hot,

I'm finally joined on the court by some of the fellas and we get it started,

Deciding on what game to play, we play hard, not for the faint hearted,

A fierce game of 21 ensued and a lot of smack was being talked,

And it only got worse when over to the court the girls walked,

They took a seat on the bleachers, all them on the top row,

At that point our game of 21 turned into a show,

Trick shots and fancy dribbling, anything to garner cheers,

From the honeys giggling now as they head down the stairs,

Of the bleachers to the fences and eventually onto the court,

Making fun on how my boys shoot and play their favorite sport,

Now there's nothing funnier than watching girls who don't play ball, play ball,

Awkward shooting, horrible dribbling and screaming, their shots never fall,

But that's a way to get close to girls in a non-creepy fashion,

Bring them into your world, introduce them to your passion,

And if they feel it, then they're feeling you and it'll all be cool,

More times than not, it's better to have girl friends than girlfriends when in school,

But any way, they end up playing keep away and it's kinda irritating,

At the chaos that ensues and to just give up and walk off the court, I'm debating,

But then Keisha gets the ball and I can't help but stop and stare,

At the girl with hazel green eyes and light brown hair,

She was wearing forest green shorts with a matching shirt with the group Menudo on it,

This girl was fine and she had the ball and it was something that I wanted,

I said "Yo, quit playin'" she just laughed at me and ran away with it,

Then she turned around and passed it to her friend, I was hoping that she stayed with it,

I just stop chasing the ball because it was almost lunch time and I was annoyed,

She messed up a perfectly good game of 21 that I could've enjoyed,

It's ok though, it was time to eat so I went to get my spot,

And if you ever had lunch in Runyon Heights Park you know it was the opposite of hot,

But whatever, it was free and guess who comes to sit across from me,

Keisha and her friends and I thought it was plain to see,

That she was feeling the kid but more than likely I was wrong,

I tried to play the shy role because that part of my game was strong,

We all talked about music and a lot of other stuff,

How one kid could jump off the swings until someone called his bluff,

So there we go, running to the swings to see him do it,

He says he could jump the highest off the swings like there's nothing to it,

We all got called back to put our plates in the trash,

Mrs. Major, the parks director, is someone you didn't want to clash,

With because she'll ban you from all activities in the park for a day,

And tell your parents and you really wouldn't have much to say,

Anyway, we run back over to the swings to see this kid Vance do this trick,

So here we all are around the swings and the crowd is getting thick,

Well it's not really a crowd, just the normal park kids hanging out,

By the swings to see what all the commotion is about,

One of the kids give Vance an underdog push and runs underneath him,

It's the best and only way to get some speed on the swings, so then,

The crowd of kids split into two groups while Vance swings in between us

The way me and Keisha keep staring, I know someone must've seen us,

So here it is, Vance swings up, and then Vance swings back,

He swings up again and staring at those hazel green eyes has gotten me off track,

He swings back one last time before dismounting up in the air,

He was way up there, his expression was one that looked as if he didn't care,

If he gets hurt or not, he was a lil' neighborhood hard rock,

He'd do anything, any dare, bad boy around the clock,

He's floating in the air which briefly broke my stare,

Comes down pretty hard but made it through to some cheers,

He even added a roll at the end to add a little flare,

One of the kids exclaim "Wow Vance, you were waaaaay up there!"

I congratulated him and then went to get my ball,

I went to trade it in for my bike, which was in the hall,

See, I couldn't have them both outside at the same time,

That was one of the rules that my Mom had designed,

Anyway, I'm riding up to the park entrance and then get off to walk it in,

No riding bikes in the park, that was considered a summer sin,

I see some kids on the benches so I go and park my bike near the fence,

I saw Keisha with her friends giggling and I got the sense,

That she wondered where I went off to because she asked "Where'd my ball go?"

I told her I traded my ball for my bike which I happen to like more, so,

"What are y'all talkin' about?" I asked her hoping to start a private conversation,

"Not much," she responded, "Going back and forth about the best radio station,"

"WBLS or KISS, it doesn't really matter much to me,"

I cut her off and said "It's WBLS all day, it's real easy to see."

Other people chime in and the conversation gets loud,

She noticed me walking to the fence, leaning on my bike all proud,

She said "I like your bike" and that made me get all cheesy,

I gotta try to keep it cool before other people see me,

"Thanks," I tell her "I think I got the best bike around,"

"Ask anyone of these kids, they know how I get down."

She smiled and looked away as if to say she knows I'm full of it,

I gotta find a way, at least today to show how cool I get,

She walked down off the benches to join the others going to Crock's,

That the neighborhood store towards the end of this block,

"Are you coming?" She asked with one hand on her hip,

"Nah," I said "I'm gonna have to pass on this trip."

"Well do you want anything?" She asked, I told her no, she responded "My treat."

What, a girl offering to buy me something, this could be sweet,

"No thanks." I told her and she ran to catch up with the others,

I chose to stay back and hang out with the brothers,

I wheel my bike over to the swings, and then lean it on the fence,

Then I got get on the swings and I'm wondering why I am feeling so tense,

I guess it has to be this girl, she has me feeling a little funny,

I would've went with her but was told not to go to the store if I lacked money,

So I'm slowly swinging on the swings and I decide to take a ride,

I go and grab my bike and calmly walk the bike outside,

Out the the park and I take off, down the street, not fast, just cruising,

There's no rhyme or reason about the path that I'm choosing,

I hit the end of the block, then turn around to come back,

I go to Otto Brehm because that's where they make the cookies at,

I go and get two because they always give us cookies for free,

I return back to the park and take a guess on who I see,

Sitting on the bleachers on the top row it was Keisha,

With some quarter waters juices and a hot slice of pizza,

"Dang girl," I said "I was just gone for a minute"

"I come back and you got a slice with extra cheese all in it"

She laughs and says that she bought me a juice,

Either I could have the grape or the orange, it's up to me to choose,

I chose the orange and thanked her and told her that she didn't have to do it,

She smiled and I between bites she said "Ain't nothing to it"

We talked for a long time and I found out some things about her,

Truthfully that whole conversation seems like a blur,

I told her that I saw her a while ago when I had that race with Shawn,

She said that she seen me that day, but as soon as she blinked, I was gone,

I laughed and I told her that I was losing at that point,

But I felt that my Huffy was faster than his and it didn't disappoint,

She told me that she was born in August "What?" I said "Me too",

"You know Leos are the freshest, there's nothing we can't do"

She laughed and that was the beginning of really good summer,

I didn't know what it was at the time but I did know I want her,

To be my girlfriend and we ended up being a couple,

Together every day, keeping my behind out of trouble,

We did a lot together at the park, made little gifts and things,

Playing basketball, playing tag, pushing each other on the swings,

And when the park would close, I'd take her for a ride,

On my bike which also led to our first kiss on the curvy slide,

Her arms around my waist as I would pedal down the block,

She would watch me play my games, my Runyon Heights Colts rock,

That was my girl and my black and gold BMX is what carried,

Us from under the big tree in the park where we got married,

I had plenty of races and daring things that I did on my bike,

Like like flying down the hill on Belknap when I lost my brakes one night,

Like chasing a van down the street that had a Pee Wee basketball team,

Called Sweet N Low from School Street who played dirty and it seems,

That when I got my first flat was around the time basketball became my first priority,

As for any free time, being on the ball court took up the majority,

I still had my girl though that lasted the rest of the summer,

But I can't say that having a flat on my BMX wasn't a bummer,

I got so many stories that I never told, some secrets that I'll always hold,

Nothing will ever beat the memory of my first BMX, black and gold!!

I Can't Remember To Forget You

Sometimes when I'm alone I wonder if you ever tend to think of me,

Or is it a distant memory that you don't even want to see,

Does it hurt when you look back or is it just forgotten?

The days I treated you like a queen to nights I treated you rotten,

Many times I tried to make up for all the mistakes that I've made,

Days I called you out your name, days that I left you home afraid,

The days I didn't bother convince you that your heart wasn't being played,

The days I saw through your façade to witness a tearful cascade,

Yeah it was easy for me to write it off as to just being young,

These words are so familiar because it's the same song I've always sung,

I've loved before you and after, just not on the same level,

I'm a little more cautious now, no longer the heartbreaking rebel,

The days to months to years that followed our breakup had me trying to realign myself,

With the girl that meant the world to me, on certain levels, help me find myself,

But it didn't work out, it's like I blew my only chance,

Too preoccupied with the frustration of not getting the last dance,

But it all worked out in the end, in weird ways unseen,

No longer have you on the brain, I'm finally over you so it seems,

I can move on now, I'm good, no longer am I alone now,

Not worried so much about the past, I'm a lil' bit strong now,

You were like a mold or a stencil that I would have other girls try to fit it,

I know I was wrong for comparing them to you, I know girl, I admit it,

I lost a lot of relationships by having them try to be another you,

How many guys know how it feels to break their own heart, girl you know I do,

I've done that and I finally realized the obvious cold fact,

That I was the reason for the split and I was never getting you back,

But I guess it's a sense of closure that has me writing this,

No more staring at the phone, no more yearning for your kiss,

No more dwelling on the past while I'm coping with the present,

You had me strung out, which made dating other girls kinda unpleasant,

They all know of you and wonder how you got such a hold of me,

To this day I still play it off like I'm not bothered by you being over me,

I still remember the slight smiles, the playful way that you laughed,

The deep conversations we had as you were in your bubble bath,

But you know out of everything, the thing that I miss so much,

The way the hairs on the back of my neck would raise just with your slightest touch,

How every time I saw you it was like the first time, days without you were like the worst times,

How even some nights I prayed to God and asked him to reverse time,

But I met someone new and she's all you were and more,

She occupies all of my thoughts so my feelings for you are no more,

She says to look forward to the future and just let the past be the past,

Because it'll eat me up inside and the times of loss are the points I won't get past,

So to be honest, when it comes to us, I just remember certain things,

I remember talks of baby names; I remember styles of wedding rings,

Our first kiss, our first fight, when you were sick I stayed and held your hand tight,

Our first date and the feeling I got when you asked me to stay the night,

Even though we just cuddled on living room couch in plain sight,

And the promises that we made to always stay in each other's life,

So as I look at it all, I actually remember more than I really should,

I remember being asked what would I give for you and replying anything I could,

I remember so much, but what else is there to do,

But to face the facts that I just can't remember to forget you,

Damn.

Teenage Love: The Remix

Here it is, the last days of summer, right before school starts,

Everyone's talking about the last movie they seen, reciting all the cool parts,

The girls are in one group, the fellas are in the other,

Made up of mostly mutual friends, some even sisters and brothers,

Well that's not totally true; there are two that have been a couple on the low,

But to save themselves some drama, they refused to put on a show,

Not that they are ashamed, they really just don't wanna hear it from all their friends,

Talk about how they're not right for each other and complain to no end,

They try to be slick and show little to interest when out in public,

Trying to play it cool, knowing that each other really loves it,

They send private messages through Facebook, sometimes an occasional tag,

In a picture with friends that they both have, so that it doesn't raise a flag,

In anybody's mind that they are secretly the newest item,

There were many times she thought "What the hell, I'll just write him",

But she just knew what her girls would say, so she never did,

Let her emotions out on Facebook saying that she's feeling the kid,

Everybody's cracking jokes and having a good time,

The wannabe cheerleaders reciting cheers, the fellas reciting rhymes,

They all compare their schedules to see if they share any of the same classes,

See who has who for first period, and the best way to duplicate hallway passes,

But it's getting late and everyone decides to go their separate ways,

Some of the girls say that they're going to Instagram what they're wearing the next day,

As both parties split up Lisa sneaks in a slight wink of her eye,

To Jay, her secret boyfriend who smirks, that's his silent reply,

She goes home and thinks about him as she's eating dinner,

She can't help but smile as she chews, thinking that she's found herself a winner,

Her Mom notices that she's been in a cheerful mood as of late,

She asks if there's a boy involved, Lisa replies "No." as she happily stares into her plate,

"There better not be!" as her Dad chimes in, away goes her grin,

He says "This is not how I want your sophomore year to begin!"

"I know Dad, I know," She says while looking at her Mom rolling her eyes,

"I need to focus on school and sports, I have no time for guys."

"That's my girl!" he replies as he grabs the plates and heads into the kitchen,

She turns to her Mom and whispers "Why is he always bitchin?"

"I get good grades, I play sports and I'm involved in all types clubs,"

"He still treats me like I'm a criminal; he still treats me like a scrub."

Her Mom cracks a smile and then she grabs her by her hand,

She whispers "There are a lot of things about your father that you just don't understand,"

"He just wants what's best for you and he feels that boys will just trip you up,"

"If you want a full ride to the college that you want, don't let a boy slip you up."

"I know ma, I know," Lisa says with exasperation as she gets up and pushes in her chair,

"Lisa," her Mom says, "We're not being hard, it's only because we care."

Lisa laughs and looks up to the ceiling and says "Well could you care a little less,"

"Between school, sports and my friends, you're just adding to my stress."

She kisses her Mom on the forehead and heads to her room and locks the door,

Picks out her outfit for tomorrow and puts her new sneakers on the floor,

Grabs her phone and checks Instagram to see what her friends are wearing tomorrow,

Because if it's flyer than what she's going to wear, from her sister she might borrow,

Some of her clothes or something but that's not even the case,

As she's looking at all those photos, she says "These girls just have no taste."

Right before she jumps in the shower, she logs onto Facebook to write a post,

Trying to be as vague as possible, "Can't wait to see the people I miss the most!"

She lets out a little chuckle as she gets her things ready for her shower,

Ready to try this new shampoo she has that smells like honey suckle flowers,

Once she's out of the shower she combs her hair, lays down and closes her eyes,

Still with that same smile on her face that she gets when she thinks about a certain guy,

6:30 am rolls around and she's ready to get the day started,

She's thinking a ponytail with curls, maybe have her hair zigzag parted,

White retro Jordan's number 3's, a Jordan jersey dress and matching purse,

Her Jumpman backpack, she eats some breakfast, drink some and juice now it's time to disperse,

She walks to her bus stop and meet up with her girlfriends,

They are all looking good, they have a reputation to uphold and,

They do it just well, as they check each other out,

One of her friends says "We're gonna run this school" her other friend says "No doubt!"

They all start laughing and slap each other five,

For now they wait on the bus because none of them has a car to drive,

Now the bus is running late but I guess that it's ok,

Because up the block, a group of boys start coming their way,

Brand new kicks and gear on and fresh haircuts,

Baggy Jeans, but not to the point that it's hanging off their butts,

They really all look good and it's obvious that they are feeling themselves,

With all this cocky stuff coming out their mouths, they're clearly not hearing themselves,

They start with all that player stuff and being really rude, thinking that they're fly,

Since when did talking to girls like that begin to be the thing to do for guys,

She sees the one that she's an attraction for on the low, who's not taking place in all the show,

Playing it cool, he just walks over and says hello,

She responds with a "Hi," but clutches her backpack because she's a little nervous,

Never really had a boyfriend, always concentrated on school so she feels she deserves this,

They keep it really short and look away, and go talk to their respective friends,

Inside she's just buggin' on how this school year is starting to begin,

The bus finally comes and they all get ready to pile on in,

She sits toward the front with her girls, he's in the back with his friends,

She still sneaks looks to the back of the bus maybe a quick lock of the eyes,

He acts like he's not into it, frontin' in front of his guys,

But he does look back gives her a quick wink,

Turns away to see if his boys seen it, it's clear that he cares what they think,

Whatever, she joins in a heated conversation that has her girls playfully going at it,

About who's going to be the first one with the balls enough to get tatted,

They finally get to school and everyone heads to their lockers to put their stuff away,

She was with these girls just last night, suddenly they have so much to say,

One is talking about her classes; one is talking about her teachers,

One is saying how they are gonna find a new spot to sit when on the bleachers,

Lisa just wants to find her locker and she does just that,

It's ironic that her locker is down the hall from Jay's and his little pack,

Of friends who are loud and obnoxious and who are always cracking jokes,

On whoever's around, from talking about your clothes to talking about your folks,

She sees Jay but just continues to put her things away,

Her heart starts to beat a little faster when she sees him start walking her way,

She has a lump in her throat which is dry and all of a sudden she has clammy hands,

She's wondering why she's feeling this way just because of the approach of her man,

Jay has a confident strut and it's one of the things that drew her interest,

He's actually wearing some of the things that she happen to like on Pinterest,

Jay goes to the water fountain but angles himself so that he can still see Lisa,

She's looking good as well, he eyes her as she's in a conversation with Teresa,

This is her best friend but a mutual friend, so he sees no problem with butting in,

"Hey 'Rese," he says "I'll see you at lunch, I'm off to 1st period gym."

"How'd you get gym 1st period," she says sarcastically, "You ain't fly!"

He responds "You know exactly how I got 1st period gym, because I'm THAT GUY!"

He runs off and Lisa cracks a smile as he vanishes within the crowd,

Teresa said, "He's just showing off, he didn't have to get that loud."

The bell rings and the girls all split up and lazily head to their classes,

The second bell that goes off is a final warning to the masses,

Lisa gets to class and finds her seat and puts phone on vibrate,

One last Facebook post, "Lovin' the first day so far, as for lunch......CAN'T WAIT!!"

There's something about the first day of school and it doesn't matter what the grade,

It's all about improving your status in school; upgrade the reputation that you made,

Fresh starts and new beginnings, clean slate, who could ask for more,

You have a whole year to prove that you're not the same as the year before,

Lunch rolls around and you can kinda feel the anticipation in the air,

It'll be like a fashion show, everyone's checking what everyone else chose to wear,

On the first day, cliques are set, some even carried over from the year prior,

If you do something stupid this day, it'll spread like wildfire,

Jay and the boys have the table along the right wall with the best view,

They see just about everything from the entrance to the restrooms,

The cheerleaders have two tables in the center of the lunchroom,

You know, because they're cheerleaders and anything less just won't do,

The football and baseball teams have the tables along the "jock" wall,

That's what they affectionately call it because everyone over there plays ball,

You got the science kids, the music groups, the weight lifters and ROTC troops,

The cool kids, the freshman, sophomores and loners quietly finish out the groups,

Seniors and juniors have cars so they go off campus to eat lunch,

They wouldn't be caught dead eating food at school, only if they're in a crunch,

Teresa and Lisa walk in the lunchroom to find a very long line,

And navigating through this one just might take some time,

Lisa decides to just go get a Pepsi from the soda machine and some chips,

From the salad bar she goes over to purchase some dip,

She hears someone banging on the tables making beats,

There's a crowd gathering around, her and Teresa hustle to find seats,

There she finds the guys kicking rhymes off the top of their head,

There are about five of them, but she's just zeroed in on one instead,

She sees Jay and she's just focused on his lips,

How he flows so effortlessly with his words and never trips,

The way he uses his hands to emphasize every word that he speaks,

The way he rocks side to side to the beat, keeps her on the edge of her seat,

It's like she's mesmerized by him, she just can't stop staring,

With her mouth wide open and she's not even caring,

Teresa nudges her to snap her out of her trance,

The beat that's coming off the table just makes her want to dance,

The guys stop rapping and the crowd returns to their seats,

Lisa figures that this would be the best time to speak,

She stays to the end and some of Jay's friends take notice,

At the way she was staring but she didn't think that he'd know this,

He walks up to Teresa and asks her if she has to take the bus home,

And if so, he'll walk with her so that she's not walking alone,

"I'm not taking the bus," said Teresa, "We're going to walk home together,"

She's gesturing toward Lisa, "And take advantage of this end of summer weather."

Lisa seems stunned but quickly shows a smile then looks away,

Jay says "Why's your friend so shy, she hasn't even said a word today."

Teresa quips "You don't worry about my girl, she's cool, just mind your business,"

"What about your boys are they gonna be coming with us?"

"Yeah I guess," says Jay, "I'll let you know by the time school ends,"

"Hopefully your friend will have more to say by then."

He laughs and walks away; Lisa just doesn't know what to say,

Teresa smiles and says "Don't mind him, he always likes to play."

They both grab their things and continue their lunch outside,

Lisa and Teresa are like two peas in a pod, always side by side,

Best friends from the 3rd grade, you always see them together,

Word around school is that if you see one, you're guaranteed to see the other,

So they get outside and take a seat on the school steps,

Teresa goes on to talk about all of the boy's and all of their reps,

Lisa just wants to know about Jay, but doesn't want to raise suspicion,

Because she really doesn't know much about him so to find out is her mission,

"What about Jay," she asks "Is he a wannnabe player too?"

"Because to me, he doesn't seem like the rest of his crew."

"Well he is, girlfriend," exclaims Teresa, "Probably the worst one,"

"I could go on for hours telling you about the things that kid has done."

"He has had girls from other schools come here to start fights,"

"He's been accused of seeing one girl in the day, and be with another one at night,"

"He has multiple cell phones and things of that nature,"

"I also heard that if you ain't giving it up, he won't date ya."

All of news that she's hearing just heard kinda made Lisa's heart drop,

But as for liking her secret boyfriend, she's not going to stop,

The lunch bell rings and the girls gather their things to go to class,

Throughout the rest of the day, the things Lisa heard, she couldn't let it pass,

She sees Jay in between classes and asks if he's going to walk with them,

He answered with a "Hell yeah, ma! At 3:00, I'll see you then."

She barely gives him a smile tells him ok and keeps it moving,

She's kind of annoyed right now and doesn't know what she's doing,

She's losing her train of thought, it's plain to see that her thoughts,

Are on the fact that she might like someone who isn't exactly what she thought,

Towards the end of school she sees her coach in the hallway and stops to chat,

It's easy to spot him from a distance; he's the only one in school that can wear a hat,

He asks about her conditioning and if she's ready for basketball tryouts,

He informs her that his daughter Sammy might even try to fly out,

From USC, she was a senior last year that did her thing,

Got a full ride to Southern Cal, during the season she put Lisa under her wing,

"Really, Sam might come back?" Lisa says with a sense of excitement,

"I can't wait to see her again; I wanna know how her first night went."

He says "Well she wants to help me out with the practices and run drills with the team,"

"Maybe she'll show you her signature drop step, because you know, that move is mean."

"Yeah," said Lisa "That would be great if I could get that move down, she was a baller,"

"Maybe when I get home, I just might have to call her."

"Do that," says her coach, "She'll love to hear from you."

"Well, I gotta go Lisa; I got a lot of things to do."

He hugs her and they both go about their business,

She gets a text on her phone and is thinking "Ok, what is this."

It was a selfie of Jay from Teresa's phone sitting on the steps outside of school,

With the text saying "Where are you, are we still walking, what, do you think you're too cool?"

That brought a little smile to Lisa's face as she hustled to her locker,

Thinking she has to play this cool, because if her friend finds out, it'll shock her,

She puts her books away and grabs her purse and book bag,

Then runs to the restroom, add some make up so she doesn't look bad,

Normally she doesn't wear makeup because she's not allowed to,

But the girls that she runs with does, so she gonna do what the crowd do,

She walks outside of the school and sees her girls and some guys,

Teresa yells, "Lisa's here!" which alerts Jay, and they lock eyes,

She's still kinda stank about what she heard over lunch,

She knows she ought to get on the bus, instead of walking home with this bunch,

"Hey" she says as she walks over to Teresa and gives her a hug,

"You all ready to leave?" she asks, and Teresa gives her a shrug,

As they all take off walking some of the guys start talking all loud,

You know how boys act when they're around other boys in a crowd,

Showing off and cracking on each other, trying to get attention,

Maybe get a tag in a post or maybe even a Twitter mention,

Teresa's just in her element; she loves all of the attention from the guys,

She's also known for being a gold digger, down for whatever love buys,

Lisa's just watching all of this as she's walking off to the side,

Her feet hurt from new shoe pain, and she secretly wants a ride,

Jay sees her and yells "Are you okay over there, why don't you come walk with us",

"I thought that was the plan so you wouldn't have to take the bus."

Lisa just keeps walking and she's annoyed that she's basically walking all alone,

Her girlfriends are all with those guys so she just messing around on her phone,

She goes on Facebook and posts "I loved the first day of school, my coach was happy to see me."

Knowing that her Mom checks her page, and that's something she'd like to see,

"Lisa," shouts Jay "What, we can't get any communication?"

They all laugh and she snaps back, "What, you too cute to be a gentleman?"

He runs over to where she's at and tugs on her book bag,

Slows her down a bit so that behind the crew, they'll lag,

"Wassup with the cold shoulder, you've been iggin' me all day,"

She stops walking so that she can look into the eyes of Jay,

"I haven't been ignoring you," she says "I'm just reacting to some news,"

"That I got at lunch that tells me that what you tell me might not be true."

"Teresa told me about how much of a player you are and how you be borrowing girls' cars,"

"Pitting one girl against the other, everyone but you gets left with emotional scars,"

"I don't think I need that in my life and like I told you once before,"

"I'm all about school and ball, and there really isn't room for anything more."

Jay looks at her and nudges her forward so that they can continue walking,

He's facing her now, but walking backwards and says "Go 'head, finish talking."

"Look," she says, "What we had this past summer, it was cool and all,"

"But basketball season is right around the corner, and this can't continue into the fall,"

"You already know how my parents are and how they are about my grades,"

"You a playa right? Go on about your life, you feelings for me it'll fade,"

Jay just looks at her, then turns around and starts walking right along beside her,

They start navigating through puddles on the ground; he holds her hand to guide her,

"Aye yo!" screams Teresa, "Don't try anything funny with my girl over there!"

Jay quips "Hey don't worry about me, worry about those tracks not falling out your hair!"

Everybody cracks up laughing and then all the jokes begin,

When it comes to cracking on each other, the girls just can't win,

Jay runs back over there to join in with his crew,

While Lisa is thinking hard about what it is that she should do,

All of the things she told Jay was just tough talk to push him away,

She really like this kid, and at the time, she didn't know what to say,

Lisa just wants to go home because her Dad gets off work soon,

And if he's there before she's there, she's going to have to sneak through the window in her room,

They finally get to her street and she thanks them all for walking along,

"Hey Lisa", Jay says, "Let me holla at ya, it won't take long."

She smiles and looks down at her sneakers as she walk over towards him,

His friends are laughing and making comments as he toys with his brim,

She grabs his hat and puts it behind her back and gives him a cute grin,

He says "Seeing our public interaction, I guess it's time for us to begin,"

"To let everyone know just what's been going on this past summer,"

"How this street kid got with a this school girl, oh yeah they'll wonder,"

"Can I have my hat back? Matter of fact you can keep it,"

"Seeing how we're going to let everyone know, it's no longer our little secret."

She tells him that the hat is hers now and that she'll see him tomorrow,

She lets him know that she's going to put something on Facebook and tag him in it so to follow,

"Alright shorty," he says "Can I get a hug or a kiss?"

She says "Boy, I don't even know you like that, you wish."

"I'll see you tomorrow, I gotta go before my Dad gets home,"

"Maybe the day after we'll exchange numbers to our phones."

Jay smiles and turns to walk away to catch up with his boys,

Lisa smiles bigger puts her hand on her head, looks to the sky to regain her poise,

She knows she can't have a boyfriend, her parents would never allow it,

But she's totally enamored with this kid, even though her heart has her vision clouded,

She knows that if she goes forward with this, she has to keep it under wraps,

She has to hurry up to get home, no time for a daydream time lapse,

As she gets closer to her home, she sees her Dad's car in the driveway,

Her mind starts racing about the things that she just might have to say,

She has to figure out what her answer's going to be when asked why she walked,

She never really lied to her parents before, honesty is all she has ever talked,

She walks up to her door and puts her key in to unlock it,

Walks in and sees her Dad with his tools out and a light socket,

He's focused and didn't even turn around to say hello, which is cool,

Because then she'll have to answer to him why she's late coming from school,

"Hi Dad," she says, "Do you need me to get you anything?"

"No baby girl," he answers, "I'm tired of fighting with this thing,"

"The lights on this lamp keep flickering, and the bulbs are always new,"

"I think I finally know how to fix this, a lil' tweak here should do."

She laughs, "I'll leave you to it, and I'm going to head to my room,"

"Don't take too long with that, you know Mom will be home soon."

She stops by the kitchen and grabs a Vitamin Water from the fridge,

An apple and some grapes hoping it'll form some sort of bridge,

To cure after school hunger pains and hold her over until dinner,

But in the meantime, she's Googling Facebook for beginners,

She has to figure out how to keep her Facebook page boyfriend free,

But also to put it out there so that everyone can see,

She private messages Teresa to see if she has any ideas to fix this issue,

Teresa's always been there to help her out, provided lots of listening time and tissue,

When she didn't make the basketball team in middle school, Teresa was the first one to know,

When her grandparents passed she was the first to get the call and responded "Lisa, say it isn't so?"

They go back a long time so the love and trust is there, no need to give a second look,

She's the only one she could ever ask about deceiving her parents on Facebook,

Lisa sends the message to Teresa saying that she wants talk about hiding things on her page,

The type of things that could for sure make her parents feel some type of rage,

Teresa messages her back, "What are you sayin' you wanna block some people, that's easy,"

"Sometimes you gotta do that, stupid folks always talking greasy,"

Lisa laughs and types back, "Lol, no that's not it. I wanna hide some things from my Mom and Dad,"

"What are you trying to hide school girl, lol," types Teresa "I just know it must be bad!!"

Lisa goes on in a long message and tells her about this guy she's been seeing on the low,

How they've been secretly been a thing on Facebook and she wants to make it public and show,

That they're a couple now that even though it'll be her first,

Boyfriend, she's intended to not make this experience her worst,

Teresa now wants to know exactly who it is she's talking about,

"I'm calling you now," she messages "This conversation just took the personal route."

Lisa smiles and seconds later her phone rings and it's her best friend,

Asking about all of the details of this mystery guy and exact day when it began,

"Don't worry about all of that," says Lisa "I just need your assistance,"

"On this Facebook issue to find the path of least resistance,"

"I gotta throw off my Mom so do you know of anyone,"

"That can help me with this, because I need this to be done,"

"Before I lose my nerve and back out, lying to my Mom, what is this about?"

"I like this boy a lot, I wish that this could go a different route,"

Teresa said that she'll call back and when she does, and that she still wants to know,

"Alright, alright, I'll fill you in a lil' later," says Lisa, "Now go!"

She hangs up with Teresa and leaves her room to see if her Mom's home yet,

She makes sure that the silent option on her phone's set,

Because she's not supposed to use the phone when she's home, only when she's out,

She wants to figure out this Facebook problem but she's still having doubts,

That she just shouldn't do all of this, put her Mom through all of this,

If she finds out, her Mom's heart will be broken due to all of this,

Just then her Mom walks in and she says hello to Lisa and gives kisses,

To her husband, she says "I've got the Chinese food if you've got the dishes!"

Lisa says "Yes, I've been wanting this for a while,"

"Have you been reading the mind of your only child?"

Lisa laughs and gets the plates, forks and spoons,

Her Dad says "Baby, I've been working on this since noon,"

"I took a half day because they really didn't need me,"

"And.....Hey Lisa, take it easy with the egg rolls, don't be greedy."

Lisa just giggles and fixes everybody's plate of food,

Puts the plates on the table and her phone goes off and asks "May I be excused?"

"I'll be right back, I have to go, umm check something,"

"Oh and also I have some paperwork for you to sign some things,"

Her Mom asks if it can all wait because they're about to eat,

Lisa respond, "Yeah, yeah sure." Knowing that you could hear the phone vibrating on the seat,

She sits down and she was able to get her phone out of her back pocket,

Ease it along the side of her leg while trying not to drop it,

She puts the phone in her shoe, that was the only thing she could do,

At the time, this dinner is the only thing she wants to make it through,

Her Mom asks about school and the classes that's she's taking,

If she like her teachers so far and the possible grades that she'll be making,

Lisa tells her about the first day and how she ran into her coach,

And how he noticed how tall she has gotten just from her approach,

Her parents go on to talk amongst themselves, so she's kinda out of the loop,

But something that they did mention made her stop stirring her egg drop soup,

"You know my friend Gary," said her Dad "Well his daughter is now expecting,"

"I guess over the summer, she went and had sex without even protecting,"

"Herself from getting pregnant, now she's has a lot to handle,"

"It spread through my job like wildfire, it's now the latest scandal."

Lisa just stops, stops stirring, stops breathing, even stops blinking,

Wondering to herself what that girl possibly was thinking,

She finally looks up only to find her Dad staring her right in the face,

"Do you know that young girl, did you know that was taking place?"

Lisa tells him no and asks them both if she could go,

To her room to get her things ready for school tomorrow,

Her Mom asks "Are you not very hungry?" Lisa tells her "That's not it,"

"Basketball season is right around the corner, and in trying to stay fit,"

"So I don't want to over indulge and have to work harder later,"

"I came off the bench last season, I'm looking to be a star player."

"That's my girl," exclaims her Dad, "Your discipline is way better than mine,"

"I could never do what you do, it usually fades over time."

"It's not easy," says Lisa "But neither was coming off the bench,"

"I'm going to work hard at it until my work out clothes are drenched."

She walks back to her room and locks the door behind her,

She starts going through her worksheets from school that were in her binder,

She thumbing through them looking for a certain one and she starts to think,

About her Facebook situation and how there has to be a link,

On how to make a secret Facebook account so she's back on Google,

She actually found some links to an answers page on Yahoo!

So she clicks the link and to her surprise it has her exact question,

She knew she wasn't the only one looking for the answers she's requesting,

One answer said that it can't be done because Facebook would eventually find out,

And lock you out of all your accounts, which would for sure cast doubt,

On Lisa's plans so she keeps looking on this page and she found one,

One person added an answer to that question and it said it could be done,

All she needs is a new email address, sign up with a fake name,

Or use your own, choose a random profile picture, something not too lame,

Don't use your location, don't allow to be tagged in any photos,

Private message all your friends and let them know what's going on so,

You won't skip a beat, all of your current friends will probably accept,

It's all relatively easy, all you have to do is just follow these steps,

This just made Lisa's night as she begins to open a second window,

She can hear her heart beating, the more she types, it crescendos,

She's getting really nervous as she stops to see if she locked her door,

And it is, but she opens it and closes it just to make sure,

She heads back to her desk to start on the new email address,

She has to come up with something, something no one would ever guess,

She tries BBallgirl, but AOL informs her that the name is already taken,

3Pointspecial, Crossthemover, is all used leaving her confidence shaken,

She doesn't know what to use and she's having second thoughts,

Instead of focusing on her attributes she starts focusing on her faults,

She comes up with a couple that were okay but again, someone has them,

She keeps striking out but then it all seems to change when,

She comes up with one that was her best offering by far,

She takes last year's basketball status and this year's hopes, and gets Pinestar,

AOL accepts this name and now she finally gets the ball rolling,

Finishes clicking this and skipping that and now she starts scrolling,

Looking for profile pictures that she could use to disguise her true identity,

She's saving images left and right hoping to stay hidden like an unplanned pregnancy,

She settles on an avatar of a female basketball player spinning the ball on her finger,

Although she's excited to get this started, thoughts of betrayal still linger,

She doesn't want to be deceitful to her parents but they would never allow,

Her to have a boyfriend, they're old school, and she lives in the here and now,

She has all the pictures she needs and minimizes the AOL window,

She opens Internet Explorer convinced that she has all the proper info,

To do this right so in the URL box she begins to type,

Facebook.com and right before she hits enter, its Teresa wanting to Skype,

No time for that as she hits enter and the Facebook login page shows up,

She fills out all of the boxes and ignoring the Skype call just caused her phone to blow up,

Teresa is relentlessly calling, texting and just won't give it a rest,

She gets another text asking if she figured it out, she replies with one word, "Yes!"

She goes and reopens the AOL box and closes that out,

Gets back on Internet Explorer and she has little to no doubt,

That she could pull this off and she ready to add the profile and cover photo,

For her new Facebook account feeling pretty bold, but still keeping this on the low, though,

She hasn't emailed or messaged her friends about the secrecy she's involved in,

She logs out of the new account and into her old one with a mass message that begins,

"Hey y'all this is Lisa and this is my alternate Facebook page and screen name,"

"You know how it is with parents, the problems they cause we all share the same,"

"So here is my new page so go and shoot me a friend request and I'll accept,

"I gotta step out sometimes and if you really need me to go in depth,"

"I'll tell ya in person, but for now check it out, same name but an avatar photo,"

"I gotta keep it secret so my parents will never know, so,"

"There you have it, oh and my new email is Pinestar@aol.com,"

"Pine, because I rode sat the bench last year, star, well, you gotta know what you are,"

"See all y'all tomorrow, don't forget to send that friend request,"

"I gotta go and as always, I wish you all the best!"

She sends the message to all of her friends and then pins that website to her taskbar,

She uses Internet Explorer for her original page and Google Chrome for Pinestar,

That ought to save her some confusion and some security if her Mom comes peeping,

Through her laptop just to see on there what her daughter's been keeping,

Right before she signs off she checks Pinestar's page and she has 43 requests,

She's accepting everyone who seems to be at peace with this transgress,

She's actually shocked and some of her friends tell her that they've had secret pages for years,

And as long as she's careful with everything, she really has nothing to fear,

She starts her first post and it states "It's a new day up in this bitch ;)"

Normally she would never curse but sometimes new freedom will make you switch,

Who you are and what you do, new found freedom is indeed a mind trip

She even adds a Life Event which states "In a relationship!"

To be continued......

The Book

The first thing I do when I wake up is check my social network,

My eyes are still blurry, maybe I should get dressed first,

Nah, I gotta see what's going on and who posted what,

It probably makes more sense to get cleaned up, yeah but,

There's something about this thing that kinda has me on the hook,

When I think about it, it's like it's a feeling that just cannot be shook,

Something about that blue tab or that blue app that's just a click away,

To hearing what all of my supposed online friends have to say,

Well, they're not really my friends, even though I have over 300 of them,

And my list continues to grow and I'll probably stop when,

I hit the 400 mark, but my drive for 5 won't let me park,

On 349, gotta get on my grind and innovate like Tony Stark,

More ways to get more likes, more friends leads to more invites,

More celebrity pages to comment on, more new links to websites,

I'll try to break down my love/hate thing I'm having to make it clearer,

Because a lot of these things will have not just me looking in the mirror,

Let's see what's going on now, Chrissy is posting relationship stuff,

Throwing subliminal shots at her boyfriend, you can tell her times are tough,

She goes to all these pages that post pictures of sayings that make you think,

That she's finally done with her boyfriend, and that she's pushed past the brink,

But you know how social networks go, with so much time to spend,

A couple of posts later.......... she'll end up loving him again,

Then you have the "Like for Jesus, keep scrolling down for Hell",

I hate seeing those posts, its freedom of speech I guess, oh well,

It's like they're the social network prophet, their drink's clearly been spiked,

You mean to tell me that I endorse the devil if your picture doesn't get liked?

I also hate the open ended post that people put on there so you can ask them what's wrong

I just wish they would just come out and say it, I don't have time for the same song,

And dance that they do when they want some attention and by chance,

If you do fall into their problem, nothing you can say will change their stance,

Drama kings and queens, their posts always seem to bore me,

Always begging for someone to ask them just to finish the story,

Anyway, they're not really wasting my time, I am by reading that mess,

And I could really care less so there's really no need to stress,

About the friend requests you get from people that just wanna be nosey,

Get all up in your business, commenting on things like they really know me,

Or the ones that's always end up sending you game invites,

They never get the point that "I don't like playing games, alright!"

Or the relationship updates that a lot of us tend to share,

I'm not concerned a bit if it's complicated or not, I don't care,

Single, married, open relationship, divorced or civil union,

I really doubt that people honestly care what it is you're doing,

Because if you put out the vibe that you don't mind getting flirted with,

You're gonna get flirted with, which can lead to online perverted gifts,

Like half naked selfies, vulgar comments that can leave you shocked,

But if you do that to someone that's not feeling you like that, will get you blocked,

Oh and don't make the mistake of clicking the "Like" button on a page,

I mean, you can if you don't mind you newsfeed leaving you enraged,

Flooded with things that you had no intention of showcasing,

Just because I like Danica Patrick doesn't mean I like all kinds of racing,

Or the children holding signs that if the get 1,000 likes, Dad will quit smoking,

Or they will get a new puppy, hey, there's nothing wrong with hoping,

Oh and while I'm at it I know some people have events coming up, duly noted,

But come on with everything you post is your party being promoted,

Some people steal your posts and pics and pass it off as their own,

I call it Facejacking, taking ideas and stuff like they were on loan,

I mean, if you're gonna take my stuff at least tag me in it so that people know,

That you got it from me, an etiquette that many rarely show,

Probably the worst thing are people whose only mission it's seems is to wreck,

The English language, those who are really in desperate need of a spell check,

They must think it's cute or something, and I truly don't understand,

Why all of their posts seem like they're trying to type short hand,

Friend requests are great until you get someone you won't accept,

Where's the "Denied" button, because honestly, as quiet as it's kept,

The "Not now" option just doesn't cut it, and they won't let it rest,

You've been denied 5 times, stop sending me damn friend requests,

I love it then I hate it, and unfortunately, I love it again,

"People you may know" uhhh maybe, friend request? Yup, send.

The Prayer

Dear God, I want to thank you for another safe day and getting me home to my family,

I'm a good guy with a complicated soul but I know you understand me,

I ask for your continued support in helping me put my family on a better financial ground,

You've gotten me this far and I know you won't let me down,

I ask for you to look after my wife with this disease that she has,

Make sure it doesn't spread any further, if you would, please give her a pass,

This family needs her around, so I'm not going to ask you for a cure,

Just know that I don't want it to progress any further then it has that's for sure,

I ask that you watch over my kids and bless them with common sense,

I mean, they are good kids in general, but you know this life, sometimes, can get intense,

Just help me guide them to make smart decisions and to keep them out of harm's way,

Let my actions show how I feel about them, more than my words can say,

I ask you to forgive me for my sins; I know I ask that of you every night,

I'm a good guy with a good heart, still struggling to fight the good fight,

You've blessed me with second chances and I could never thank you enough,

For being the one I turned to when my life & times got really rough,

I ask that you bless the families of murdered and abducted children,

The sexually assaulted, those who lost their homes to fires and floods and lives to villains,

I ask that you bless my family, cousins, aunts, uncles, nephews and nieces,

Help them fulfill their dreams and attain whatever their hearts pleases,

Even though we're not as close as I'd like, just know that it's still all love,

And that I'll always be there for whatever, if push comes to shove,

Kiss my Mom for me, hug my grandparents and bless all of my friends,

In the name of the Father, Son and Holy Spirit, Amen.

Acknowledgements

I want to thank my family for shaping me into the person that I am today. The initial groundwork was laid by my Parents and Grand Parents, so I want to thank them for that. I want to thank my children Jordan and Jaelyn for being a constant reminder to try to do the right things. My brothers Tony and Steven and my sister Renee, for sticking it out when times got rough. My wife Jessica for always being there.

I want to send an extra special thanks to Chelsie McFall, because if it weren't for you, I wouldn't have even thought about putting this book out. Thanks for sparking the idea of just putting it out there.

Contact me at:

caesarlyricaltas@aol.com

www.facebook.com/lyricalthoughtsandstories

www.ingramcontent.com/pod-product-compliance
Lightning Source LLC
Chambersburg PA
CBHW060402050426
42449CB00009B/1859